THE WISDOM OF
J. Marvin Spiegelman, Ph.D.

Volume I - Selected Writings

Other Titles by Dr. Israel Regardie

A Garden of Pomegranates
A Practical Guide to Geomantic Divination - A Small Gem
Attract and Use Healing Energy - A Small Gem
Be Yourself - A Guide to Relaxation and Health
Ceremonial Magic
Dr. Israel Regardie's Definitive Work on Aleister Crowley,
  The Eye In The Triangle
Healing Energy, Prayer and Relaxation
How To Make and Use Talismans - A Small Gem
My Rosicrucian Adventure
Mysticism, Psychology and Oedipus - A Small Gem
Teachers of Fulfillment
The Art and Meaning of Magic - A Small Gem
The Body-Mind Connection, A Path to Well-Being - A Small Gem
The Complete Golden Dawn System of Magic
The Complete Golden Dawn System of Magic Book 1 - Ltd. Edition
The Complete Golden Dawn System of Magic Book 2 - Ltd. Edition
The Complete Golden Dawn System of Magic - The Black Edition
The Eye in the Triangle: An Interpretation of Aleister Crowley
The Golden Dawn Audio CDs, Vol. 1, Vol. 2, and Vol. 3
The Legend of Aleister Crowley
The Magic of Israel Regardie
The Middle Pillar
The Philosopher's Stone
The Portable Complete Golden Dawn System of Magic
The Tree of Life
The Wisdom of Israel Regardie - Vol. I
  Selected Introductions, Prefaces and Forewords
The Wisdom of Israel Regardie - Vol. II
  Selected Essays and Commentaries
The Wisdom of Israel Regardie - Vol. III
  Selected Articles, Introductions, Prefaces and Forewords
What You Should Know About the Golden Dawn
Aha! (Dr. Israel Regardie and Aleister Crowley)
Roll Away The Stone/The Herb Dangerous
  (Dr. Israel Regardie and Aleister Crowley)

MANY OF OUR TITLES AVAILABLE ON KINDLE!
Please visit our website at http://www.newfalcon.com

Other Titles by J. Marvin Spiegelman, Ph.D.

A Modern Jew in Search of Soul

Buddhism and Jungian Psychology

Catholicism and Jungian Psychology

Hinduism and Jungian Psychology

Mysticism, Psychology and Oedipus - A Small Gem

Protestanism and Jungian Psychology

Psychotherapy and Religion at the Millennium and Beyond

Psychotherapy as a Mutual Process

Reich, Jung, Regardie & Me - The Unhealed Healer

Rider, Haggard, Henry Miller & I - The Unpublished Writer

Sufism, Islam and Jungian Psychology

The Knight - A Small Gem

The Nymphomaniac

The Quest - Further Adventures in the Unconcious

The Tree of Life - Paths in Jungian Individuation

The Wisdom of J. Marvin Speigelman
   Volume I - Selected Writings

The Wisdom of J. Marvin Speigelman
   Volume II - Psychology and Religion

MANY OF OUR TITLES AVAILABLE ON KINDLE!
Please visit our website at http://www.newfalcon.com

Copyright © 2021 New Falcon Publications

All rights reserved. No part of this book,
in part or in whole, may be reproduced, transmitted,
or utilized, in any form or by any means, electronic or mechanical,
including photocopying, recording, or by any information storage
and retrieval system, without permission in writing
from the publisher, except for brief quotations
in critical articles, books and reviews.

ISBN 13: 978-1-56184-501-9
ISBN 10: 1-56184-501-9

New Falcon Publications First Edition 2021

Cover Painting and book design by Delfina Marquez Noe

The paper used in this publication meets the minimum requirements
of the American National Standard for Permanence of
Paper for Printed Library Materials Z39.48-1984

Printed in USA

NEW FALCON PUBLICATIONS
2046 Hillhurst Avenue
Los Angeles, CA 90027
www.newfalcon.com
email: info@newfalcon.com

THE WISDOM OF
J. Marvin Spiegelman, Ph.D.

෨ ෨ ෨

Volume I: Selected Writings

Introduction by Mary L. Marquez

NEW FALCON PUBLICATIONS
LOS ANGELES, CALIFORNIA, U.S.A.

Introduction

The Wisdom of J. Marvin Spiegelman, Ph.D.
Volume I: Selected Writings
By Mary L. Marquez, B.A.

"Be the man through whom you wish to influence others. Mere talk has always been counted hollow, and there is no trick, however artful, by which this simple truth can be evaded in the long run... the fact of being convinced and not the thing we are convinced of-that is what has always, and at all times, worked."

—C.G. Jung

Collected Works, Vol. 16, "Problems of Modern Psychology," p. 166-7, 1929.

The Wisdom of J. Marvin Spiegelman, Ph.D., Volume I: Selected Writings is a variety of rich, insightful writings which invite Jungian analysts, psychotherapists, and all other interested readers alike into Dr. Spiegelman's own Jungian journey. It is a journey of inquiry into what is helpful to other psychotherapist in training through the experiences and development of fellow colleagues' own techniques resultant from psychotherapy as a mutual process. Psychotherapy does not occur in separateness.

Dr. Spiegelman also explores the impact of suffering on the analysts and how it affects their lives. He addresses the continuous confrontation of the suffering of others and states, "the suffering becomes our own". Some of the issues he addresses are anxiety, depression, sex, money, and the paradox of therapists who feel alienated in a group, but simultaneously can pursue individuation and self-realization.

In continuing Dr. Spiegelman's intriguing, but grounded journey he shares his own experiences of active imagination through the utilization of Jungian archetypes, and an amalgamation of myths, religions, spirituality, dreams, and fantasy. He names this combination of psychological knowledge and active imagination: Psycho-mythology: a new literary genre. He shares that his own stories emerged from active imagination (stories from the unconscious) and that this type of expression (s) according to Jung are expressions of the individual psyche. He makes it clear that they are not a diagnostic tool, but part of the individuation process.

In conclusion, *The Wisdom of J. Marvin Spiegelman, Ph.D., Volume I: Selected Writings,* most notably provide us not only with his innovative psychological search and insights, but with his own humanity; a participant in his own individuation and wholeness:

L'ENVOI

And what, at last do the Gods select?
And what, at last do centers effect?
Why Psyche, of course, in her butterfly state
Yes, Psyche, of course, love's soul and love's mate

It is Psyche and Eros who go through the changes
It is Psyche and Eros who flew through the ranges
Of center to center, straight up and straight down
Of center to center, each glows with a crown

The Lord speaks in Gods and in animals, too
The Lord, most of all, speaks in me and in you
For we are the vessel of God's transformation
Yes, we are the vessel, no group and no nation

The soul and the spirit unite in the flesh
The soul and the spirit delight and enmesh
In man and in woman, alone and together
In man and in woman, God's stone and God's feather

For God is both matter and spirit, at end
For God is both changing and permanent
In centers is He, for soul and for wife
In centers is She, behold Tree of Life

This is the end of the work, Him
This is the end of the work, Hymn
This is the end of the work, Her
This is the end of the work, Sir
This is the end of the work, It
This is the end of the work, Writ

—J. Marvin Spiegelman, Ph.D.
Jungian Psychology and the Passions of the Soul
p. 434, 1989

Table of Contents

Introduction by Mary L. Marquez	v
Preface to *Jungian Analysts: Their Visions and Vulnerabilities*	1
The Impact of Suffering and Self-Disclosure on the Life of the Analyst	5
Introduction to *Psychotherapy as a Mutual Process*	43
Notes from the Underground - A View of Love and Religion From A Psychotherapist's Cave (1969)	59
Introduction to *Jungian Psychology and The Passions of the Soul*	77
Preface and Introduction to *Reich, Jung, Regardie & Me - The Unhealed Healer*	89
Introduction to *Rider Haggard, Henry Miller & I - The Unpublished Writer*	119
Active Imagination and Story-Writing: Individuation and Art	125
Introduction to *The Tree of Life*	139
Psycho-Mythology, A New Literary Genre	143
Introduction to *The Quest*	151
A Capsule of *The Tree*	157
Part V An East-West Tree of Life and Hymns	167

Mutus Liber from C.G. Jung's
Psychology of Transference

A Preface to
JUNGIAN ANALYSTS:
THEIR VISIONS AND VULNERABILITIES
New Falcon Publications, First Edition, 1988

It is with pleasure (and with appreciation to the contributors) that I present this book to those readers who might welcome it as a glimpse into the sincere reflections of experienced analysts. It is the kind of book that I wish had been available to read when I first began doing psychotherapy in 1951 or even when I began doing analysis under supervision, during the "control" phase of training, in Zürich in 1957. Every neophyte psychotherapist is anxious to "do it right"–whatever that means–and is uncertain as to how to proceed, no matter how much personal analysis he or she has had or how many training courses. The reason for this is the psychotherapy, in contrast with Behavior Modification, has to do with the soul. It is an art and a sensitivity to individuals, not a technique nor a science. All that one learns–history of symbols, mythology and religion, case studies, psychiatry and psychology, the arts, and from physical and biological sciences–is only background for the moment when one is confronted with the individuality of that suffering person who presents himself for therapy or analysis. All one's training helps, but it is of great benefit–even essential–to get the accumulated wisdom of one's senior colleagues, how they have approached the work and what they have learned through experience. It is in this way that the new therapist can glean hints, can supplement his own inner work with the comparative information that he longs for. To learn an art, one needs to examine the art of others. And that is what this book is about: a dozen senior Jungian analysts responded to the question as to how they go about doing what they do and what they have learned about it over the years.

The book began when I was writing about my own approach to analysis, realizing that it would be useful to compare the experience of others. To try and get the insights of senior Jungian analyst on paper, therefore, I took the membership list of the International Association of Analytical Psychology in 1959–the year that I joined the Association and the second-to-last-year when Jung was still alive–and sent out an announcement of the task at hand to approximately 50 of the 150 members then listed, along with two others who graduated from the C.G. Jung Institute Zürich shortly afterward. I knew that these analysts had experienced Jung directly (a desideratum of selection), and that most of the others had not, or had died. To be sure that no one who was qualified to be included would be missed, I also placed an announcement in the current (1985) bulletin of the International Association of Analytical Psychology, which went to some one thousand members. No further response resulted from this announcement, but of the fifty notices sent personally, fourteen sent regrets; I was informed that two others had died; and sixteen agreed to participate. Eighteen, or 36%, did not respond at all. At last, a dozen analysts submitted papers and these are herein presented. In order to make this work of more use of people in training, I asked Dr. Joe McNair, a particularly able candidate in the Los Angeles training program, to read the papers, raise questions and make comments. His and my remarks were then sent to the contributors, who were kind enough to respond. Since McNair and I are still involved in the training process, I asked Fordham and Samuels of England to comment on my paper also. The results follow. At the end of the contributions there is an "Epilogue," in which Dr. McNair describes his experiences in doing this work. I think that readers, particularly people in training, will enjoy his overview of his experience of this "opus."

Finally, there is a brief autobiographical section at the conclusion of the book, wherein the contributors were asked to describe their educational background and the nature of their contact with Jung.

I am impressed with the seriousness and depth of the presentations of my colleagues. All but two (von der Heydt and Ziegler) were known to me personally; many of them were also students during my own years at the C.G. Jung Institute Zürich in the last 1950s. All the same, the fact that this dozen hail from three continents, five countries, and at least eight cities, suggests that there is considerable difference among them. Three of them (Fordham, von der Heydt and Wheelwright) are "first-generation." All twelve experienced Jung in some way; yet the reader may be startled and pleased (as was I) at their differences as well as their similarities. I think that Jung would be delighted to see that individuation has been served.

I wish to thank these colleagues for their generous response to the project, and to Falcon Press for seeing the value of its publication. I also want to acknowledge the permission of the C.G. Jung Institute of San Francisco to reprint Dr. Wheelwright's contribution, which appeared as part of his own book, *ST. GEORGE AND THE DANDELION*, published by them. A summary version of my own paper was presented at a national Jungian meeting in Boston in the fall of 1985. I hope that other colleagues will be inspired to similar endeavors. Advancement in our "art" will surely be enhanced by the sincere and reflective reportage of those who have been devotedly committed to its practice. Finally, I wish to express my appreciation to those analysts, teachers and colleagues who have contributed to my own growth in the field. As a bare minimum among these, I want to mention C.A. Meier, Marie-

Louise von Franz, Liliane Frey, Rivkah Kluger and, in memoriam, Max Zeller, Bruno Klopfer, Hilde Kirsch, and Margaret McLean. If I add, as teachers, Barbara Hannah, Jolande Jacobi and James Kirsch, I mention only a minimum and neglect many others. To this august list, I would add, also in memoriam, the name of the secretary of the Institute during my years in Zürich, Alice Maurer, helper and good friend. Above all, the name of C.G. Jung–whose genius has been a beacon and even a life-saving gift to so many–is rightfully acknowledged in the title itself.

J. Marvin Spiegelman
Studio City, California
Winter 1987-1988

THE IMPACT OF SUFFERING AND SELF-DISCLOSURE ON THE LIFE OF THE ANALYST

A chapter from *Jungian Analysts: Their Visions and Vulnerabilities*
New Falcon Publications, First Edition, 1988

In the bathroom of my office hangs a poster portraying a life-size statue of a nude woman, before which stands a man wearing only a hat, coat and shoes, his back toward the observer. He bares himself to the statue, and the poster carries the inscription, "Expose yourself to Art." I have certainly been troubled by the issue of self-disclosure. Over the years, I have had a number of dreams of being in a public situation with either the wrong clothes or no clothes, and I have spent lots of time trying to sort out this issue of my persona in some decent way, without a huge amount of success.

One resolution of this issue, to expose to and for art, has resulted in several books of fiction I have written, and my style, even in scholarly articles, has been personal and often self-revelatory. In the following comments, I shall both reveal and conceal, for that theme, I maintain, along with suffering, is a chief feature of the life of the analyst, particularly in our work.

Patients come to us and reveal their secrets, their lives, their concerns, and we listen carefully, thoughtfully, and appreciatively, trying to be non-judgemental, if we can. Even if we can not, we have exposed our own shadows and secrets to our analysts enough so that we are less inclined, by and large, to condemn patients, if not each other.

This self-revelation of patients, we realize, is ultimately Self-realization with a capital S, since we understand that this exploration, thus begun and continued becomes an arena in which the Self is gradually made manifest. Jung has taught us that it is not only the Self of the patient which is being revealed, but it is also the analyst's Self which is constellated and we are not only "in" the work with patients, but are required to reveal ourselves as well. For myself, I have found that what needs to be revealed are not facts and secrets about my life–but what I am thinking and feeling in relation to the patient, since the unconscious mobilized in both parties. Therefore, the Selves are ultimately exposed, to one degree or another.

Not long ago, I added another little card, next to the poster I mentioned earlier, given to me by my wife for a birthday. On this card is shown a rather meek, elderly gentleman wearing a proper suit and carrying an umbrella. He glances rather startledly at a woman whose back is toward us. She is a fulsome creature, wearing a luxury fur coat, and she bares herself to this shy soul.

This card balances the picture. The two, together, express my views about the process of analysis being, ultimately, a mutual one, in which both parties are exposed to each other, and more importantly, to the unconscious itself. This fact, peculiar to our profession, has far-reaching effects upon us. I shall be noting these effects in the further course of this paper. Now, however, I wish to examine the second theme of the paper, that of suffering.

We can approach this theme, perhaps, by asking: What is it that makes the life of an analyst different from that of a chiropractor, astronaut, interior decorator or chef? The first thing that comes to mind is that we are connected with, fixed on, devoted to, suffering. We are totally and intimately confronted by the suffering of those who come to us, since they do not usually bring–at least at the outset–their joy, achievements and delights. This strange involvement with suffering already makes our lives different from the last three occupations, but not different from the chiropractor and, for that matter, from the physician, nurse, social worker or clergyman. These other healers, however, have quite a different outlook on human suffering. They are armed with techniques to alleviate pain or ameliorate the environmental strictures which cause or aggravate the pain. Physicians and nurses are skilled in the precise administration of drugs and procedures which cure or soften. Social workers and priests are allied with institutions which make life-in-pain more bearable. Clergy, furthermore, have instruments and sacraments of belief and practice which give them direct access to helpful forces. Should these interventions prove unsuccessful, they do not consider themselves to blame, nor do their constituents.

Only "shrinks" can not shrink from nor evade the direct, powerless encounter with suffering. We are armed with our concepts, to be sure, and the strength resulting from endless years of training-analysis, but ultimately, as Jung has taught us, we are equipped only with our Selves. We encounter this suffering as both symptom and event, as condition and person, and our central question is always, "What are we–and they–going to do about it?" The answer for us is always individual, although the repeated encounter with this dilemma profoundly affects us. In order to understand the life of the analyst, we need to comprehend this endless confrontation with suffering, a feature which contributes mightily to our own "deformation professionelle."

How are we to approach this issue of suffering and what does it do to our lives? We all know that confession is good for the soul. We encourage our patients to fully and deeply express all that makes them suffer, to associate to it, to round it out, and together with us, to examine the causes and purposes of such pain. This work usually alleviates the suffering or ultimately provides meaning to make it bearable. It also can transform it. We are in the position of a caring and intelligent friend, but we are also knowledgeable and skilled in communicating non-judgementally and with some objectivity. Furthermore, as Jungians, we are committed to the view that the ultimate healer and authority lies within the person. We address our efforts to link this sufferer with his inner world, and we try to read the messages of the Self of the patient, in dream and fantasy, which leads toward healing and understanding.

But what does this repeated exposure to suffering do to us? Particularly when our efforts, understanding, and compassion are insufficient? We, too, are infected, as Jung pointed out, and our own suffering inevitably comes into the picture, both induced and activated, both similar to that of the patient and different. Finally, it is or becomes our own.

Could this fact account for the high suicide rate among psychiatrists? Perhaps it underlies the common wisdom that those who work in the area of mental health do not generally possess much of it themselves. We try to find off such suffering, of course, both consciously and unconsciously, but the resultant rigidity and closed-offedness, as described by Guggenbuhl in his *POWER AND THE HELPING PROFESSIONS*, is not attractive either. In short, the issue hinges on what we call the transference, seen by many of us as not just the projections of the patient on the therapist, but as the unconscious commingling of the psyches, in which the archetypes are constellated and the analyst is affected as well as the patient. All this we know from Jung, who also told us that there must be some reason for us to have chosen such a dour and bleak vocation, that our psyches must need it. Indeed, we are all very much aware of the proffered image of the "wounded healer" and that we even heal from our own wounds opened up in the work.

I have never been happy with this image of the "wounded healer." I am aware that I am, indeed, continually wounded by patients and their psyches, that I help in the healing by finding my wholeness in the face of the fragmentation and distress which patients bring and which divides me, even splits me. The image is too dark and heavy, however, and leaves out the healing effects of joy and laughter.

We will remain with the issue of suffering, however, and examine how this effects our lives in a number of areas. I will address eight of these, and then return to our general themes of suffering and self-disclosure and the myths which underlie them. The areas which I have chosen are anxiety, depression, aggression, sex, money, alienation, community and religion. A large handful, naturally, and perhaps too much to include, but I shall be offering reflections on two grounds: First, I have always had a number of patients who have been therapists, so I speak not only idiosyncratically. Second, my own suffering as a result of forces external to the work has been relatively mild, compared to many other people. So I think that I can speak of the suffering of the therapist which is a consequence of the work itself and of the personality of the therapist which is a consequence of the work itself and of the personality of the therapist who, by either fate or choice, is immersed in such a vocation. Indeed, since my subjective impression is that I have suffered a lot in this work, I wonder how some of my colleagues, less blessed than myself in the areas of relationship and security, survive the assaults on the soul which our work brings.

ANXIETY

The first step in our eight-fold path of examination of the suffering of the therapist is that of anxiety. My own experience of anxiety, outside of the therapeutic hour, has been that of it being attached to other topics of my chosen list, namely aggression, sex, money, alienation, community and religion. I have only rarely experienced—outside of analysis—what we called in my Rorschach days "free-floating anxiety," or the nameless dread of which Kierkegaard speaks. Yet I have had patients, of course, who have suffered from this condition, and such a dread has indeed frequently manifested in the work. Jung believed that anxiety was associated with the numinous: dread and awe are the necessary concomitants of facing the gods. I recall Madame Jolande Jacobi, in a course at the Institute in Zürich in the late 1950s, solemnly intoning that such anxiety arises as a consequence of not being in touch with one's shadow. If your shadow is with you, providing the earthly grounding of its instinctiveness, for example, your anxiety will change to a specific fear, a realistic apprehension of present danger. A true statement, this, an done that we unconsciously assent to when we encourage patients to "go with the anxiety," to see where it leads and to what it refers. Name the god, s it were, awakening during the analytic hour? Are we alert, we rightly ask ourselves? Are we connected, doing the "right thing"? Is this patient going to be all right, will he/she quit or commit suicide? Now, as I contemplate this anxiety of my patient and experience my powerlessness to alleviate it, to interpret it, even cope with it, my own anxiety arises by induction. As I experience this, I think, shall I reveal that I, too, am anxious, powerless, helpless? Will this self-disclosure aggravate the patient, make him/her feel even more helpless and also feel that I can not assist or even cope with the nameless fear? Or if I do reveal my own anxiety, will this be beneficial, alleviate the condition by a sharing, by an indication that I can stand it, endure it? Or, if I do disclose, will it be the feeling of anxiety itself, or will I also reveal that I am afraid that I can not help, that I will be abandoned by the person who, perhaps, is feeling the very fear of abandonment which is now assaulting me?

In my own analytical stance of "mutual process," in the belief that the archetype is now constellated between us, I will likely reveal any or all of the above and wait for the reaction. And the result? Sometimes very helpful, sometimes not. Sometimes this self-disclosure on my part leads to a deepening, a capacity to move onward and more meaningfully, with a therapeutic effect. Sometimes, however, I am greeted by—and I think now of a particular patient—a look at me from previously downcast eyes, with non-understanding, a further dread and a sense that I, too, can not help him, just as no other therapist could.

So, with this patient I am powerless and even the confession of our mutual powerlessness makes things worse. I then suggest that we both ask or pray together for the source of this dread to reveal itself here in the room. And now, this rationalist who has been successful in his life but in his sixties is nearly broken and defeated, is so fearful of praying together and, probably, finds this erstwhile rational therapist to be a superstitious and dangerous fool, that he wants to bolt. Yet he also has a little hope and wants to please me. I feel the same thing, I say, in a further orgy of self-disclosure, and the hour ends. Soon, not in that session but in several more, he terminates the therapy, and I feel like the fool. Now, many months later, as I write, I feel the need to telephone him and find out if what I said above was true for him. So, I call and he is delighted to hear from me. Yes, he is still surviving, just the same as before, only just barely. He is with a previous therapist, one who gave him drugs. Yes, I was right that the demon was just too much and that he was even more terrified of being together in prayer. He feels that he should have stuck it out. But that is not why he left. He ended because there was just too much gloom and doom and in our relationship, nothing upbeat. No, it isn't better now; the demon of which he was afraid is still there, it neither leaves him nor kills him. We share a few words of mutual appreciation and hang up. So, here I am with my paper, once more, my own anxiety alleviated by a connection with him and by the healing power of self-revelation. The demon-dog, dark and unforgiving, relents for one moment and my ex-patient is grateful for the care and contact and I am grateful that I need not feel guilty for the failure, nor feel abandoned. So, whose therapy is it? For whom do we do this work?

I turn now, to my colleagues, toward whom I direct these words, and acknowledge that it is the self-disclosure which seems to be at issue here, whether successful or not, whether it assists the patient or not. I conclude from this that what is mobilized in such events is, indeed, the god itself, which we dread. It is the darkness of the dread, and the dark side of the Self which is being revealed. The self-disclosure about which we are ambivalent as professionals is actually disclosure of the Self (capital S). This is what is at stake in our work. We reveal and conceal, just as the Self is revealed and concealed. Our struggle is to find the right attitude with which to address this revelation. The Self-manifestation of the images of the divine, which usually remain in the background for others, haunt us. The aspects of totality which want to be seen and incarnated also defy all our efforts at approach, whether we placate, command, cooperate or submit. Ultimately, I think, with each patient, if we go deep enough, we discover aspects of this god of Self, and anxiety is just such a condition for its encounter.

I wonder, then, if my other anxieties, apart from the therapeutic vessel where it is induced, are also manifestations of the god? Is the god which I fear out there in the world the same one? When I am anxious over money, over abandonment, over performance, do I experience the self-revelation of the god? The same demon that plagued the patient with whom I failed? Am I, too, merely hanging on, surviving the onslaught, neither relieved nor dying? At times it seems that way. But I also find, unlike my patient, that my capacity to kneel to the higher power, to regard it as Other and greater, to do all I can with my ego, but also to surrender this ego is what brings relief, meaning, continuity. Do I teach this to my patients? I suspect that I do.

What is the difference between anxiety considered the therapeutic process and that encountered in the workaday world? Everyone suffers anxiety about money, performance, security, and we all dread the unknown. But how we handle it alone and with friends and loved ones is a different matter than how we do this with patients. With the latter, we are participatory, we are induced, we are willing victims. We are part of that stoked alchemical process which even heats up the feared and rejected content. Some colleagues, mostly Freudians, want to increase anxiety, turn up the heat, providing motivation for greater and more sincere work. I do not share that view. The god comes of its own accord. Just work away and the unconscious, if so inclined, will appear. The hard part, as it was with my anxiety-ridden patient who had positive dreams and deep dread, is to integrate it, to endure it, to survive it.

And that is how our lives as analysts are different from others: we are partners in the plague. We submit to the darkness, to the "emotional plague" as Reich called it, willingly, with consciousness, even gladly, because this, we think, will heal or transform or bring more light. What is more, we do this because it is our calling, our vocation, or life. This does make us strange in the eyes of the world, and makes it difficult for us to communicate what we do, how we are. This makes us, too, like scientists and prostitutes, not ordinary. And, as with the vocations just mentioned, we are admired and despised, sought after and feared.

DEPRESSION

This psychological condition is, in my experience, the most typical and frequent form of psycho-pathology found among our fellow therapists. Most of us experience down-goings and despairs in the course of the work, and more than other professionals do. Witness: the high suicide-rate among psychiatrists. Witness: the later works of Freud, Adler, Reich, and in a more profound and worked-out way—as for instance in *ANSWER TO JOB*–Jung. Pessimism and the problem of evil is the lot of the advanced worker in the vineyards of the soul. So, too, has this been my own most typical psycho-pathology, particularly since the age of forty. How many mornings have I awakened in darkness, gloomy and distressed! Everything seems laden with uncertainty and pain. Why is this so? I remember telling Michael Fordham that his work was certainly brilliant, but it usually left me feeling depressed. He responded, heartily, that he thought this was a good thing, since I was too high up in the air and needed to be brought back to earth. My fiction-writing, for example, was unfoundedly optimistic. Well, he had read only my first psycho-mythology book, *THE TREE*, which is surely upbeat, but he had not read my book called, *THE FAILURES*, a story of an unhealed healer, an unpublished writer, an empty teacher, and an unfrocked priest, all of whom go for healing to a powerless magician.

Yet Fordham had a point. Many therapists, Jungians particularly, tend to be intuitives or intellectuals and we are, indeed, high up or in the head, not enough connected with the body and the earth. But, then, what about the most important body-therapist and theorist, Wilhelm Reich? He ended up with a very pessimistic attitude, as shown in his book *REICH SPEAKS OF FREUD*, if not downright mad. And what of Freud and his feelings of "discontent" and "disillusion"? Non-Jungians are bleak, too.

One reason for this depressive and disillusioning condition is to be found in what our colleague Robert Bosnak, of Amsterdam and Boston, has discovered in our images of inferiority. Starting with Freud's first "Irma" dream–the archetypal beginning of the work of analysts–Bosnak shows us that it is the analyst's image of inferiority, defeat and incompetence which dogs us endlessly in our work. His paper was the first I ever read which spoke to the condition I have usually had, not so much in therapy itself (although I do occasionally experience it there also), but whenever reading Freudian-style work. Feelings of inferiority, failure, and incompetence come with that reductive attitude, I believe. It is, all the same, true. We are archetypally conditioned to experience this lamentable condition. But the writings of Jung, I find, with its synthetic attitude toward darkness, provides the necessary complement to the reduction. Not only is the analyst's anima, as in Irma, badly treated, too much for us, and sick, she is also, as in Jung's anima of his doctoral dissertation, a medium for the depths, fascinating and revealing.

However we conceive of this depression which dogs most of us, how do we deal with it? Following the Jungian procedure, we go down with it, we let it speak, we follow the movement of the soul into the depths. But many of our patients can not or will not do this. It is not their way, especially in the earlier years of the work. So, then, what do we do, or suggest to them? Well, we burn it out, in the American method, through activity: jogging, swimming, exercise. Here the image of coping with the "nigredo" is to burn away the dankness and heaviness of Saturn, which sometimes works, sometimes not. How different, say, from the attitude toward depression taken by the Asian! One Japanese psychiatrist who worked with me told me that the treatment of choice for depression in his country was rest, to be quiet, to retreat and to allow nature to restore energy and wholeness. How different from us!

I am reminded of the poster suggested by an American monk to contrast the western and eastern viewpoints. It said": "Don't just do something, the Buddha said, stand there!"

In my own experience, all of these methods–rest, active imagination, and consciously moving away from the dark moods–do help the condition. All are right at times and are ineffective or inappropriate at others. How do we know which and when, and how do we know when to ask our medical colleagues for help with drugs for those patients with whom none of these is effective? Well, we don't know, although there are books about depression and increasing knowledge about its physiological concomitants and antecedents.

What we do know is that we therapists experience more of it than do other professionals. Is this through the induction I have spoken of? Or the initial condition of our psyches which attracts us to the work in the first place? Or the necessary compensation to our heights and intuitive soarings? As it is with all the treatment modes, so are all the explanations true. Furthermore, we seem to experience more failure than do physicians or lawyers, more frustration in achieving goals of wholeness and creativity. We are willy-nilly tied to extreme ambiguity and uncertainty in our work. Very little is certain and even that is always relative to that particular individual who enters into our offices and our psyches. The blessings and curses of individuality, like that for art, depend on the soul and its achievement. But how do we gauge the latter? Are we like van Gogh, geniuses who produce great work and are not recognized, or like Boucher, precious and talented, successful but shallow? How many of us look to highly recognized or more successful colleagues, particularly those from other schools, and see them as shallow, or catering to the public triviality?

That competitive and envious shadow is to be solved, I discovered, by sacrificing it, abjuring it, consciously, in the outer world. Give up the competition and embrace the simple life. I suspect that many of us have come to such a solution privately. We go to work, come home to family and friends, read our books, write papers, tend our gardens, look forward to those weeks of vacation in the mountains and seashore, and are content. Work and Love, said Freud, and resolve competition that way. Yes. In this, we are like many other people, yet we come to this, I think, out of the heat and drama of our work, the deadness and vitality of the analytic process, in which the alchemy is secret and contained, for we can not even talk much to others about what we do.

No wonder we are inferior and superior, and no wonder so many of us opt for the simple life outside, to compensate the complexity and uncertainty of the inside—that is, the inside of our offices and the inside of our souls. We are specialists in the darkness of the soul, and in that we can join no other vocation that I can think of, not even that of most clergy. We are more like monks or hermits in that regard, but we are neither totally alone nor in groups, as they are. We are with an "other" and with each "other" who appears. What a profession! What a blessing and what a curse! No wonder we seem strange, and no wonder the simple life is so attractive to many of us.

The answer then—or, at least, my answer—to the depression evoked in our work, is the simple life. Brought down from ambition, greed and competition, to joys of the simple life. Brought down, too, to the divine darkness which enters into our work and wants to be included in our lives, lived as an undercurrent to our simplicity.

AGGRESSION

We move, now, as a depth psychological might be expected to, from depression to aggression. Have we not been told that the former is a repression of the latter? And that the expression of anger and its concomitants is the cure of the same? Well, yes and no. We do know, from Reich, that anxiety and sexuality are mutually exclusive, physiologically and psychologically, but I am not at all sure that depression and aggression are in the same polar connection. I have spent lots of time on a Reichian couch, yelling and hitting, which has been relieving, but that, in itself, did not "cure" depression as much as the "simple life' has. Nor do I generally have much trouble being in touch with my own aggression and being able to verbalize it in fantasy. These capacities to imagine and verbalize, however, have been only partly effective against what I conceive as my greater problem, that of muscular tension.

Muscular tension, in turn, in my opinion, is very much a consequence of our work. Sitting there, day after day, attending to the psyche of the other, is certainly "contra naturum" and requires lots of physical exercise and non-concentration on others as an antidote, but even that unnaturalness is not the cause of this stress. Rather, I think, that which produces stress is the endless alertness required of us, the perpetual attention to what is happening in self and other, so that mere relaxation and unconsciousness is a luxury indulged in all too rarely. Furthermore, the poison of the process seeps into us; the unacknowledged rage and aggression of our patients in what claws at us from below and from behind, bombards us hourly, daily, weekly, yearly. After some years, I found, our bodies, so assaulted and alerted, become tense, rigid, inflexible. Tennis and running won't do it, although they help. Even Reichian therapy and conscious connection with the body is not enough either, although very helpful to me.

I really do not know any remedy for the stress and muscular tension, although we each have many methods for coping. But what are we to do about the restraint of our natural aggression? Not that we need to hit patients or yell at them, but we might need to say to passive-aggressive folks, "Wake up and acknowledge your negativity and hostility, damn it! And even if we did, it would not help much, even though it could conceivably be consciousness-bringing for a particular patient. No, the poisons which seep into us go deeper, and our constraint against running away, or against natural reactions–fight or flight–even if we allow ourselves verbal expression in the hour, are such that we can never overcome the "analytical stance." That analytical stance, unnatural in the extreme, is full-attention, alertness, care for the other, and restraint of our natural reactions and movements, all in the name of compassion and consciousness.

Nor would we have it any other way. That "contra naturam" is what we do and what we teach. Our release come from insight and union of soul. They also come when we can effectively be natural and whole with our aggression with the patient. But still, what do we do about the body and this unnaturalness? Luckily for most of us, analysts are not by nature inclined to be particularly aggressive physically or even strongly athletic. Most of us are contented with our week-end tennis, swimming and walking. We add to that by going into nature when we can, and being healed of these poisons of the soul by the Great Mother Herself, as we hike in Her precincts, smell the trees and revel in the silences.

But the tensions persist anyway and Jungians, in contrast to Reichians, are said to be insufficiently "in the body," or are even seen as "dead." At some conventions, alas, I have seen what they mean. But I have also been at a Reichian convention or two and I am not impressed with what I have elsewhere called a "P.E." approach to life.

The reasons for this persistence of tension, as I have said, are not only the restraint and alertness of the therapist, but also the endless taking-in of the poisons, via the unconscious in particular. Transference does indeed "absorb" us, and we are absorbed into this endless "nigredo" and mercurial poison, no matter how much we are aware. I think that we do rather well, by and large, considering the extent and nature of our work. Those of us who have worked a long period of time in a mental hospital will know what I mean. The poisons of the soul infect the atmosphere to the extent that one can hardly tell patient from therapist in such institutions after a few years. Nor is this limited to the insane, in my opinion. The darknesses of the psyche revealed every day in the newspaper and confronted on the freeways of social intercourse are compounded in our rooms by perfectly decent people, including ourselves. The devils provoke our consciousness; our consciousness provokes the devils. The cure is in the process, but is never fully effected. When one speaks of the "wounded healer," I think of it as residing in my tense muscles, rather than in unhealed complexes, and I think that I am not alone in this. Perhaps the muscles are where the complexes reside.

Mars, then, is insufficiently served in our work, since we can only accept him in the soul. We do not jump, fight, yell, run away; nor do we sit in a sweat box, sleep–or most of all–turn off consciousness in those intense daily hours. Intensity without activity, and poison without antidote: those are the deformations that really count in this baleful work, a field more dismal even than economics.

I am still working on this problem which, for me, is to be even more aware of the body in my work and even more conscious of what is happening therein and to attend to it. I try to bring in my aggressive reactions, verbally, as much as possible, and to be "natural." I seek mutuality in the work with aggressive energies. Still, I search for new answers. I have weekly deep-tissue Ayurvedic massage, have experimented with bio-feedback. Colleagues do other things, such as Feldenkrais, as well as stretches (as I do) and running.

Women therapists seem to have less of a problem with this matter than men do. Maybe they can relax better or are less aggressive by nature or by role. I would be glad to know why. Perhaps this is one compensation for them for the centuries of oppression by that same masculine aggression and why they have lived longer and, by and large, happier lives.

However we view the issue of "dealing with the poisons" on a personal, subjective basis, the implications of the transference and the resultant alchemical work with patients can not successfully be denied. Ultimately, we need to confront ourselves and our patients that these poisons are being extruded "into the room" and are shared as an alchemical "third" between the two partners. My own response to this dilemma, which Jung recognized in his book, *PSYCHOLOGY OF THE TRANSFERENCE*, has been to embrace what I call "mutual process"–the recognition that ultimately both partners are effected by the archetype and they work consciously and openly together to transform these poisons and gifts of Mercurius. The word used by Joe McNair for this process is "metabolize" and I think it is appropriate. This archetypal element arise from and goes into the very cells of the body, particularly since we are committed to a work of the soul and spirit and deal in image and word. The body gets it, and it is, in my opinion, only when we acknowledge and share these bodily reactions that there results a mutual "metabolization" of these transpersonal poisons and gifts.

SEXUALITY

When we turn from aggression to sexuality, we have to say "more of same" to all that we have already said about aggression. It seems that we male therapists suffer more from this general inhibition against acting-out than do our female colleagues. We are stimulated and restrained as well. We are seduced and become seducers. We are privy to all the sexual secrets and are challenged beyond wits end. If Mars is frustrated by analytic work and makes us pay the price in muscular tension, Aphrodite is both worshipped and denied, and she is compelled to submit to being appreciated in the form of her son, Eros. We serve soul and spiritual union, not the flesh.

Furthermore, when we discover that we suffer more from the unexpressed, indirect form of aggression manifested by our patients than from open hostility, we also recognize that it is the silent seduction and stimulation that goes on in the therapeutic relation which causes havoc. If I am "turned on," as they say, is it because I am feeling and experiencing something in the patient or in myself alone? And, if I acknowledge this openly, am I going to be misunderstood as making an overture to sexual acting-out, or am I being unconsciously seductive? And, if the patient opens up desire, lust, and love, may I react honestly and directly with what I experience–verbally, of course–or should I interpret, or merely acknowledge. Most of these possibilities (except interpretation) occur in non-analytic relationships, it is true, but in analysis they are heightened, carry more weight and implication.

My own resolution of the dilemma is to be open about not only the stimulation and arousal, but to present the accompanying fantasy, with the expressed intention of offering these as reactions, and inviting the patient to report his/her reactions and fantasies. With my viewpoint of mutual process, I believe that body reactions, including aggression and sexuality, are usually archetypal responses and, if I am open and show the way of dealing with them by example, I am aiding in the direction of integration, rather than repression, evasion or acting-out, I preface such self-revelation with a statement of the nature of our analytic commitment to consciousness and enhancing the capacity to love–not to acting-out, nor to love affairs, etc. When the limitations of the work are mutually accepted, then both parties can open up to what the unconscious brings in when it is, indeed, mutual. It is in this way, in my experience, that the poison of the unexpressed, unresolved sexual and aggressive fantasies can be fruitfully worked on and transformed.

But one is always in danger of misunderstanding. I think, now, of a woman I worked with who had a negative father problem. I liked her, but did not find her particularly attractive. After a time, however, I became aware of sexual feelings about and toward her. I hesitatingly told her so, and she was utterly startled, since she had no such feelings toward me. She reluctantly accepted these things, however, and, in time, I thought of this as a kind of ambivalent Eros coming through me which would repair the damage done by the father's disregard and rejection of this woman when she had reached adolescence. I was both bringing up the rejected and repressed and teaching her how to deal with it by listening to and expressing her own honest reactions. At times, however, I felt like a dirty old man.

One day, at the time of the notoriety of some child-abuse cases in our area, I had such feelings again, and then I said, "Perhaps I should open up a nursery school?" We both laughed uproariously. It was not long after that when a memory of her being abused as a child returned and the dissociated sexuality made perfect sense, both as a "return of the repressed" and as a "healing of the wound (of rejection and invasion) of the father." This was a healing event. Would this have occurred if I had kept my mouth shut? I do not know. But that is our dilemma.

My own experience of the analytic work is that I am soon divided into my opposites by the patient and what he/she brings to the sessions. I often feel as if my "left hand" is open to the taboos of the soul, my own included, and my "right hand" maintains the protective, parenting, connecting energy, with both "hands" being necessary. My advantage is that I sit in the middle of these and can move toward or report either of these directions or fantasies, and not be possessed by nor identified with either of them. I continue until wholeness is achieved. I have to add, however, the word "usually," or one of Jung's favorite Latin quotations, "deo concedente," for such is our need and trust when serving the healing god, the Self, as manifested in the analytic work.

What sort of life is this, for the analyst to talk about, stir up and express, though limitedly, this lustful and tabooed aspect of the psyche every day, with many people? Are we not secret Don Juans, or dirty old men? Yes, certainly, for these are "rejecta" of the psyche which intrude themselves into the work as the darker aspects of Eros, clamoring to be accepted, healed, integrated. And they must be included, but deprived of their destructive violating aspects. Spirit and flesh, morality and desire are thereby re-united and the initial splitting effect of the patient, mirroring his/her own split, becomes healed in the relationship we call transference. Poison, once more, is included and dissolved through a healing connection.

This is strange work, is it not? Here we are, rather ordinary-looking men and women, engaged in a secret sex and aggressive life, like our brother and sister hustlers, prostitutes. Perhaps we are like the "enlightened one" in the last of the ten Zen Ox-herding pictures, consorting with wine-bibers, butchers and other rejected ones and, as the commentary to the picture says, we and they are "all converted into Buddhas." No wonder we are secret heroes and heroines, as well as secret hustlers and "devils," because, indeed, we aim to be secret Buddhas, or at least to serve such divine images.

I find it difficult to understand how those colleagues of ours who do not have a religious attitude deal with these upsurges of lust, desire, and violence, as they bubble up in the "vas," the vessel of the analytic work. If we did not have a religious attitude, how could we (I) possibly do this work? Badly, I would imagine. But then I don't know what other gods are being served, consciously or unconsciously, by colleagues. I am personally convinced that some god is being served, whether one is aware of it or not, and we are compelled, all of us, to find out which one and how.

Again, what strange work this is. Not even clergy are required to do this? Now, does it suit us? I think so, since we not only redeem the psyche in this work, we are ourselves continually redeemed thereby. But to whom but you, my colleagues, can I say this? It sounds so inflated. Yet it is clear that we are quite ordinary, all the same. Another paradox to accept.

MONEY

Money is a topic for us which may be even more charged and filled with taboo than sexuality and aggression. Everyone knows, of course, that we charge entirely too much for our time, that all we do is listen, that therapy has little effect. Besides that, are we not caretakers of the soul? Should we not be generous, loving and giving, a kind of Dr. Christian of the psyche? If not, we ought to be.

Now, such a collective image of what psychotherapists are or ought to be is bad enough for us, but if we add the suffering of patients about money, then we are in further trouble. How many of them feel cheated or deprived by unloving parents or a hostile world? And how many of these believe, somewhere deep down, that somebody—namely, the therapist—should make up for these lacks and deprivations? To charge for our time is understandable, but we should be non-mercenary, unmaterialistic, and self-sacrificing.

How is an analyst to deal with these images and expectations? First, we try to make them conscious. Even when they are made conscious, does that settle the matter? I remember working with a psychotherapist who told me that throughout his previous long

Freudian analysis he had the mildly subliminal hope and belief that his analyst was saving up all his checks and would give them back to him at the end of the work. With me, his image was more that of an insurance policy. If he came and exposed his weaknesses and failings with me, then these would not destroy him in the outside world. The issue became, how much was he willing to pay for that service, and when would he get these things fulfilled elsewhere for less money? This financial attitude toward therapy came from a capable, generous, very conscious man. Just like me. We, too, are just as generous, caring, socially responsible, and devoted to service as was my analysand, but are also just as frightened, insecure, envious and greedy as the next man. We have worked at these things and are conscious, but money itself is such a charged and ambivalent symbol that one could write a psychology with that as a center as much as with our more usual Eros and Thanatos psychologies.

We all share the consciousness of money as a symbol of security, value, prestige, personal worth, power, love, and even connected with the Self. But why do I become so enraged when patients not only do not pay me, but do not even apologize for not doing so? Why am I driven to murderous thoughts by such cheating, when with other losses I can be more philosophical? And why, too, do I worry when my practice drops, get chagrined when I hear that former students and colleagues have fuller practices or get more for their services than I do? Is this only the usual envy and competition? Am I alone in such emotional financial intensity? I don't think so.

Surely we analysts, like our patients and everybody else, suffer the usual problems of money, such as the need for security or power that I mentioned above. We also suffer from the unreal expectations of patients and the collective. I am of the opinion, however, that we Jungians have an additional suffering in this area just because we believe that we are serving the Self. I have discovered that in this belief of system, I welcome each new patient as, somehow, sent by God. I am there for his/her development as well as my own, and the problems that are presented are just the ones that I need to deal with at this time, even if I don't like it. That, of course, makes my working life and each patient quite meaningful for me. Jung said that this was a good attitude for us to have. The other part of this belief, I have discovered, is that somewhere I have the expectation that the Self should take care of me. Since I am devoted to doing the work of the Self, both within my psyche and "in the world," then patients should be provided who can pay me enough for the livelihood of my family and myself. If the Self wants me to do this work, it should see to it, by golly, that I survive in it! If not, then I, like fallen-away priests and nuns, have lost my "vocation"!

No wonder, then, that I am so enraged when patients do not pay, and don't even acknowledge that they owe me. They are denying the Self for me. The imagined penalty for that, in my mind, is death! Is it a wonder, then, when they—less conscious than I—expect me to work for nothing? Should I not be father and mother, even an agent of the Self for them, too? What to do, then, with this painful insight?

I am reminded of a dream I had some years ago, which still lies in the back of my mind about many things, including money. In this dream, I was walking across a bridge to a futuristic city when a crippled beggar, bodiless and seated on a sort of skateboard, comes to me and announces that he is God. I nod and offer to buy him a drink at the kiosk there. As I acknowledge him, this self-proclaimed God-figure grows a body and is quite whole. After we toast each other with wine, he holds out his palms to me, from which flow a huge number of gold and silver coins from every country and time. End of dream.

This, then, is how I understand the complexity about money: The Self is both a beggar and a provider; it wants to incarnate into my life and needs my recognition. When I do so and share a relationship of spirit, then all the values and achievements of the ages–God expressing Himself/Herself throughout history and life–are vouchsafed me. But I can never forget that God is beggar as well as giver and that I, as a carrier of such an ever-incarnating content, am also beggar and giver. I can not escape this dilemma, but perhaps the insight can make me less murderous on the one hand, nor destroyed on the other.

A curious thing just happened. As I was writing the foregoing lines, a patient called and announced that she did owe me money, although in the last session she denied it. She was going to send the check by mail today. God does provide! But I also need to remember that one of the most common lies told is, "the check is in the mail"!

ALIENATION

This word was more popular among intellectuals and students in the 1950 than it is today, along with the concept of "organization man." Perhaps the reason it is less popular today is that alienation is more widespread. Movies and the arts no longer glorify and console the man who is different from the crowd, who goes against the pack. Instead, they look to virtues and values of the past, of the community of the faithful farmers, the shared communion, ethnic solidarity. We are shown that communion because we lack it so much. Almost everybody feels alone in a hostile, uncaring world.

How does the analyst figure in this? We are always alienated and still are. We are "strangers in a strange land'; even the old word for our profession as healers of the mentally ill makes us "alienists." Jung told us the following, when he wrote about alchemy: the one who embarks on the individuation process finds himself alone, isolated, different from his surroundings and in possession of a secret which keeps him apart. He must work long and hard and deep to once again find his link with that collective world outside, and he must find it by going to equivalent lengths to the collective world inside.

We are, then, strangers, but friends to the patients who come to us, who themselves feel like strangers in the world. And how does this endless befriending of the stranger who comes to us effect us in the world? We are more strangers than ever, unable to engage in small talk. We often are rotten group participators, awkward and suspicious in social gatherings, guarded with our colleagues. Perhaps I paint too dark a picture and describe only myself and some others; but I venture to predict that not a few of those who see or hear these words will recognize themselves in the description.

Why is this so? Is it because of the individuation process? Or because our profession is a peculiar one and kept apart by projection and agreement? Yes, this is true, but other people are embarked on individuation and belong to peculiar professions without being especially alienated, such as astronauts, deep sea divers, and oil-well cappers. The reason, therefore, lies elsewhere. I believe, once more, that it lies in our concern with suffering and our play of self-disclosure. The person who is endlessly involved with hearing secrets, telling secrets, guarding secrets, being open and being closed, endlessly reflecting on what is going on in the background, is bound to be peculiar fellow and one who is shunned as well as courted. Shamen have few friends.

How many times I remember going to parties and when the usual questions as to my occupation came up there were snorts and jokes, petitionings for advice, opening up of problems in a corner, or not-too-subtle hostility. That was years ago. Nowadays, along with the alienation of everybody, everyone also has been to a psychotherapist or is going to one, so the novelty has worn off. It is not the ordinary fellow in other fields who is alienated from us, it is we who are alienated from him. And this just because we do this strange work of reveal-conceal, of suffering, and it effects us in the ways that I have mentioned. Since we serve the mentally ill, so are we seen as mentally ill. And, if our patients are not particularly mentally ill, still, we are branded with the label. Who can listen all day to such stuff? Who listens? We all know the jokes and stories, like these, and we all know how impossible it is to share what we really do and how we are, even amongst ourselves, let alone with other citizens.

What, then are we to do? Jung's answer, of course, is that the deepening connection with the collective unconscious at first alienates us, but later finds us once more not only connected with our fellow humans, but also to plants and animals and stones. Sometimes, however, we analysts are better connected to plants and stones. Sometimes, however, we analysts are better connected to plants and stones than to social life, and are better nourished thereby. It was Jung, too, who said that after thirty-five every man is like a lonely ship who blinks to other ships, but goes about on his own voyage. He was connected deeply, but not too personally, I think, except with a very few. It is probably not different for us. Jung had his outer collective, however, as few of us have, and even our Swiss colleague, Adolf Guggenbuhl, has addressed this isolation and alienation among us, espousing friendship as an answer to it.

For myself, the answer lies partly in friendship, but also in being more open in the analytic work, in enjoying and appreciating family, in spending lots of time in nature. Many answers and no answer, because this alienation problem leads directly to the next item on our eight-fold path of the issue of the suffering of the analyst, namely Community.

COMMUNITY

Carol Shahin has aptly described the Jungian community as a "village for people who could not remain in the village." That remark goes a long way to account for the fact that Jungian groups often split, that internecine squabbles and power plays are just as prevalent among us as in any political party. One might have thought that our penchant for integrating the shadow would have made us less quarrelsome or mutually rejecting. And for those of us who have thought that our penchant for integrating the shadow would have made us less quarrelsome or mutually rejecting. And for those of us who have even less invested in the Jungian or any collective, as such, there is apartness, "ships passing in the night." I have discovered that such a community-denigrating attitude in even built-in among Jungians generally.

Since I returned to membership in the Los Angeles Society a few years ago, I have found that almost every new graduate goes through a final darkness and frustration with the administration or some authority and comes out with the feeling that he or she would do just as well, or even better, by not being a member at all. Not only is this an unexpected outcome, but it seems to be even a desired one in some ways. In the background is the dictum, "Don't project the Self onto the Society," or any society for that matter.

Now, who can fault this advice? Certainly not I, who has had rough treatment from a Jungian collective in the past, and treats the current re-connection as an opportunity to work out my own shadow in relationship to social life. This distrust exists for most of my colleagues. Many have expressed to me their frustration and disrespect for our Society life, yet all somehow try to do what they can. My own experience is that I can find some satisfactory mode of connection with almost any member of our group on an individual basis, but as a collective, this is more difficult and frustrating. My chats with Jungians from other communities, by and large, reveal something similar.

What a paradox! All these individuation-pursuing and self-realization-promoting people have a difficult time being with each other, except on an individual basis! It would seem that we lack, on a group level, the kind of vessel that analysis itself provides, whereby consciousness, truthfulness and relationship are deeply served. Nor are we likely to find it very readily. Group therapy will not do it, as attested by the experiments of analysts and trainees from various places and times. Nor is there much desire to find or create such a vessel, since Jung thought it hopeless, really. The Jung Club of Zürich, for example, was seen as a "battlefield," according to Franz Riklin, a place to encounter your shadow, but one goes home to work it out. I have been forced to conclude that he and Jung were right about groups, in general.

But what community, and what do we analysts do about it? The answer is, not much. There are professional meetings and, as the number of Jungians increases, there is more variety and possibility of intellectual sharing, but kinship—such as it is—reduces still further. That is a fact, I believe, and one to further the suffering of the analyst. Where are the causes to serve, the parties to support, the truths to espouse? Mostly in the inner work, in the analytic structure, and in one's requirements of personal process. At best, we discover the "ecclesia spiritualis" of like-minded people, apart from collectives.

We discover our membership in the hidden community of seekers. If we are lucky, we find our compensations in a more greatly appreciated marital, family and friendship life. Yet we are deeply alone, making our link with the depths of the inner collective and looking for ways to manifest or connect in the world. Jung was both fortunate and capable in having sufficient depth and complexity to "give back" to the outer collective what he received from within, and to find, even in his lifetime, a sufficient resonance to enable him to go on. The rest of us have to do with less, although we also do not have to undergo the kind of hell he underwent, for example, in writing his **ANSWER TO JOB**.

Each of us carries his/her own process, but we do not have communal vessel of equivalent value for further work in the transformation of our collective darkness. Yet the condition of the world obviously requires such a thing. If Jung is right, the only answer for collective darkness is for the individual to work on his own, and to suffer the splits and lacks as incarnated by the Self in her/his own soul. That we must do anyway. In the future, however, with the increase in the number of extraverts who are attracted to Jungian psychology, there may be some creative contribution to our dilemma which will show a way of collective work which does not violate the individual, yet values group work, too. We who could not stay in the village find that the village we have joined is hardly a village at all!

RELIGION

The step from the issue of community to that of religion is a short one, indeed, and very much parallel to it. How many analysts are active members of a religious community? How many even attend services of any denomination with any regularity? About as many, I would suppose, as are active in community life! We are as introverted and atypical when it comes to religion as when we face community.

I used to think that this was a good thing; I shared the usual banalities about not being interested in "organized religion." By the time I had completed my training and had gone much deeper into the psyche, however, I changed and felt that it was important to have some connection with my religion of origin, that the "given"– as van der Leeuw had put it–was just as important as the "possible." I had concluded that the chief transition events of human life–birth, initiation, marriage and death–were all social phenomena, requiring ritual and a link with the community and religion of my inheritance. I fulfilled this precept for myself, my wife and children. I even added further "observance" of ritual for the chief holidays of the year (national as well as religious), as well as our regular Friday night prayers and family service of ushering in the Sabbath. All this was important just because my personal myth was ecumenical and transcended the religion of my birth to include several others, as well as being a religion of the psyche. I suspect that most of my colleagues have felt something similar, since even those who were clergy to start with end up being more therapist than spiritual counselor.

Yet, since most of us are far from immersed in community religious life, just as we are estranged from general community life, we suffer this apartness. Our individuation offers us symbolic understanding and even appreciation, but we are lacking, all the same. We do not, by and large, share the sacraments or behavioral laws which provide our fellow institutionally religious the succor and satisfaction of enactment and fulfillment. Our religious life comes from our relation to the Self, an ongoing dialogue within, which is sometimes shared in outer events and with others, but it rarely can sustain the kind of mutual worship that is the rightful inheritance of humanity at large.

The loss is severe and causes a suffering which sets us apart from how humanity has always been. We are almost as non-observant as agnostics, yet we are at least as religious as the most intensely devoted practitioners. Few of us can abide being a member of congregation. Our discrepancy militates against it. Some of us, for example, Edward Eddinger and, before him, Esther Harding, think that Jungian psychology is itself a "new dispensation." And most of us think that Jung has indeed ushered in a new consciousness which is a "quantum" leap over the past. But we are not, luckily, like the members of a new sect who have found the "truth" and want to foist it on others. We are too well aware that we endlessly struggle to find and live our own truth and we respect others need and right to do the same. But the alienation from community, and particularly religious community, is a serious suffering for us.

For the past several years, I have been leading what I call a "psycho-ecumenical group" composed of clergy who are also therapists. They include rabbis, priests, nuns and ministers, all of whom have had Jungian analysis. We have met to give papers, to demonstrate rituals, to discuss issues, to share in religious holidays. Some in this group have even said that it is easier to share certain religious doubts and struggles with each other than with the clergy of their own community. I find this group, which meets about eight times a year, to be a very important one for me. It gives some outer form to my own inner ecumenical myth, as well as helps me maintain connections with friends I might otherwise not see. This has been one resolution of my dilemma of lack of community.

Another resolution of this lack has been to attend high holiday services at a local hospital, rituals led by a rabbi who is also a psychologist and a good friend of mine. I thereby keep my connection with tradition and maintain an individual relationship. These, plus family observance, make me a most fortunate person, I believe, yet I still feel that gap, that lack of organic connection with community and community religion which, I think, is part of the alienated condition of our time. M.L. von Franz has been of the opinion that the Self wants us to be strong enough to stand alone, and I think that she is right. Yet we suffer this deprivation, since the Self is also a deeply manifold being and process which years for kinship connection on an outer collective level as well.

In the section on Money, I related a dream I had in which the Self appeared as a crippled beggar, gradually taking on body as I acknowledged him and our relationship. During the same week that I had that dream, another one came to me in which I was informed that God's body constituted the entire universe, that it was like a worm biting its own tail, that its organs were composed of all the galactic systems and planets, and that all life constituted the cells of This Being. Furthermore, I was told that this Being breathed in and out in a vast harmony, and that those cells (or beings) lucky enough to be located at the places where this breathing occurred had mystical experiences.

My dream said nothing new about the apprehension of the divine. It has been frequently noted that we are all One, and that God is One in that multiplicity of existence. Yet the difference was that I dreamed it, it happened to me personally, and it compensated that other image of God that I had, earlier in the week, which emphasized my particularity. I think that the second dream, the more collective one, made a truth real for me, but did not indicate how this was to be lived. I also think that this is the problem of "the many," that of multiplicity of images, to be resolved in the next five hundred years perhaps, the time that Jung told our colleague, Max Zeller, it would take to form the "new religion." That "new religion," I believe, will not replace any of the older ones, any more than Christianity has replaced Judaism, or Buddhism has replaced Hinduism. Yet one hopes that a balm will then be provided which our suffering souls need so badly. This will not happen for us, of course, who live now in that transition time, but we can still rejoice in having a glimpse of what is to come.

DISCUSSION

The foregoing reflections have revolved about two themes, as I mentioned at the outset. These have been self-disclosure and suffering. To round out our discussion, I think it valuable to see these issues from an archetypal perspective and for this purpose I have selected, from among other possible choices, the relation between Teiresias and the Goddess Athena for the theme of nakedness and self-disclosure.

Teiresias, you will recall, was a true prophet and visionary among the Greeks, being the one, for example, who warned about the violation of the incest taboo and prophesied several aspects of the Oedipus tale. He gained his prophetic capacity, it is related, as a consequence of inadvertently glimpsing Athena unclothed. This Goddess of culture and consciousness, born out of the head of Zeus, was deeply offended at being seen naked by Teiresias and blinded him. She recompensed him, afterwards, by giving him inner vision and the capacity to hear the gods. This same Teiresias had also been party to another event which he did not seek, when he chanced to see two snakes coupling. Attacked by them, he slew the female and was turned into a woman. After seven years, during which he lived as a harlot, he again saw snakes coupling and was attacked by them. This time, he slew the male, and resumed his masculinity.

Our seer, the mythographer Kerenyi tells us, "saw things one does not normally see," and was both honored and punished thereby. He saw the nakedness of the Goddess, her secret Self, the naked truth that lies behind the bringing of culture and consciousness. Athena, we remember, was the one who assisted Prometheus in achieving the divine fire. She is on the side of civilization, to be sure, yet to see her true nakedness–the secrets which lie behind the advancement of consciousness, as we see them in our consulting rooms–is to be blinded to the outer world as others know it. The recompense is to have increased powers of intuition and to see into the depths. We, like Teiresias, witness the breaking of taboos and the nakedness, not only of the human psyche, but also of the gods, as revealed in our work.

We also witness the union of the snakes–that symbol of divine healing–and, more than most people, we are compelled to experience our inner contrasexual opposite, male and female. For this, too, we are handsomely paid. In all this, we are serving the divine in a feminine aspect, that of the expansion of consciousness and the advancement of civilization. We do this, I believe, like Teiresias, just because we happened to "be there" when the Goddess made her appearance. We surely do more than this–which is to say that other aspects of the divine principle, such as Aphrodite and Eros, are being manifested–but it is the nakedness which is of concern right now. I would add that even though the Goddess punishes Teiresias for the hubris of seeing her, she also desires this exposure, since she is kind to him, giving him her best gift. Even Zeus and Hera look to him for authority, when they demand his expertise to resolve their quarrel as to who has more pleasure in sex, male or female. I hope it is not disrespectful to suggest that here is even a root metaphor of marriage counseling!

I would conclude from the foregoing that the gods are ambivalent about us humans, both wanting us to see and punishing us for this. Here, perhaps, lies the deeper reason for the theme of self-disclosure, which is so central in our endeavors. I would say that what is disclosed in our work is the Self, both that of patient and therapist, but also transcending both. The Self is being incarnated and disclosed, and the aim, just as Athena supports, is the advancement of consciousness. We are honored and punished thereby.

This leads to our second theme, that of suffering. An archetypal basis behind this theme, one that I choose to discuss here, comes from a dream and vision that I had a few months after beginning my own analysis at Christmas time in 1950. In it, a divine child was being born, and was attended by three new wise men, but these were a Jewish rabbi, A Christian priest, and a Buddhist priest. I did not know it then, fortunately, but this anticipated birth of the "anthropos" would be accompanied for me by these three images which are deeply related to the theme of suffering.

The Christian image, of course, that of the crucifixion of Christ, is centrally concerned with the suffering of God and man as the Self enters into the human condition. Jung has been his most profound, perhaps, in describing this event in *ANSWER TO JOB*. The central tenet in Buddhism, Duhka, the condition of suffering or dis-ease, is to be overcome by following the eight-fold path of right living, leading to the experience of the Self. And, it is no secret that Judaism, while not espousing the path of suffering as the way to the divine, has been a chief recipient of such agony during its entire history.

My dream and vision reported these attendants to the birth and now, thirty-five years later, I can acknowledge that this has been my fate–to cope with the suffering of my patients and myself as this ecumenical birth of the "anthropos" is ushered in at the end of the Piscean aeon. All three views–of the incarnation of the divine, of the endurance and transcendence of the opposites, and of the personal relationship with God as both an inner and outer fact–have permeated my own analytical work. I venture to suggest that some variant of these has affected my colleagues as well.

So, then, our suffering, perhaps, is not in vain and is itself the kind of penalty that Teiresias and Prometheus, to say nothing of Jesus and Buddha, paid with so dearly. In Judaism there is a tradition that there are, at any one time on the earth, a number of "just men," "Melamed Vovnikim," who suffer particularly because they carry the burden of the god-head. It is even greater suffering that some of them do not even know that they do this. I believe that the twenty-four men of that tradition are being added to in increasing numbers during the present generations and that we Jungian analysts are better off if we consciously realize that even to see the divine in manifestation is to be party to that suffering. The rewards are of greater consciousness and the realization of being co-creators in the vast evolutionary process which we glimpse with such awe. It is no wonder, then, that we are so burdened and uplifted by what goes on in the ordinary little rooms in which we conduct our analytic work.

Comment by Fordham on Spiegelman's Contribution

Dear Spiegelman,

Your paper has arrived. I eagerly read it and read it again. I respect the way you struggle with your conflicts and problems and wish you good luck with them but they are not mine: I do not suffer much with my patients and many of my patients do not suffer much either, indeed if they can do so productively I think that the analysis is drawing to a close. Nor do I find disclosure a problem. Let me describe an occasion when I did disclose something I have a patient who has changed his time from 9 a.m. on a Monday morning to 8:15. Twice I had expected him at 9. On each occasion, I was in my dressing gown when he arrived and he saw me thus attired. I let him in and dressed in about five minutes. When I came down he was silent but we succeeded in doing some work on that; he felt neglected, not wanted and so on. At one point he said he thought I should be on the couch and start my analysis by him. He changed the subject but towards the end of the interview I said that I did not think my failure was related to him so much as my age and difficulty in getting up in the morning. Nothing very grand about that disclosure.

What you do seems to me not so much analysis as confrontation therapy. I think most of your disclosures would have got digested and given the form of an interpretation.

But these discussions are much too brief to assess our agreements and differences over technique and it would be possible to get down to brass tacks only by submitting each other's cases to supervision by the other. Alas, not possible.

I do think it important not to get competitive and think each of our methods is the right one. I do think that what you do is sincere and I respect it, and I wish you well with it. But as far as myself, I would not act as you evidently do, sometimes at least.

With best wishes,
M.F.

Rejoinder by Spiegelman to Comment by Fordham

Dear Fordham,

Many thanks for your honest response. I liked your example, but it is, as you recognize, a far cry from what I would regard as "self-disclosure." Our differences seem to reside in what we consider important to analyze. You think of my work as "confrontation therapy"; I think of yours as dominated by the child archetype. On my side, what I analyze are dreams, and the relationship, as manifested in mutual reactions. You analyze the person. I believe that our differences represent not only personal variants but, like the "founders," we represent different analytic attitudes which could, maybe should, be more carefully compared. Alas, we can not, but perhaps someone, reading our material here, will be motivated to go further with such comparisons. Actually, many other comparisons can also be made from the contributors to the present volume. Our differences are softened, I think, in the mutual appreciation of the sincerity with which we approach the work, and our mutual respect, as well. Many thanks for your contributions to our field and to this book.

Sincerely,
J.M.S.

Comment by Andrews Samuel to Spiegelman's Contribution

Spiegelman is exposing the wound that drives him and showing how, after considerable distillation, his experience and suffering during the course of an analysis can be put at the service of the patient's individuation. We have tended to split conceptions of analysis as a two-person interaction from versions of it which stress the inner journey. My feeling is that this is a pity and this paper approaches the paradox of oneness co-existing with boundary in analysis; how "I" am only constellates in relation to "you." I was also struck by the way Spiegelman returns again and again to the centrality of the body in the analytical experience.

Marvin Spiegelman has asked me to add a brief paragraph about myself. In spite of a background in the theatre, I formed the desire to be an analyst very early–in my late teens. The reason I became a Jungian is rather unedifying. All the other training bodies to which I replied rejected me as being too young. The Society of Analytical Psychology was the only one not to reply at all. One day, while taking a stroll in central London, I "found myself" in Devonshire Place, the street in which the SAP's headquarters were then located. Not knowing the number, I asked at one of the houses and then knocked at the SAP's door. The office staff found my letter; they were not particularly surprised that nothing had been done about it. I was in the process of asking them what to do next when a voice piped up from the corner: "I'm on the professional committee–if you've got an hour to spare I could see you now because my consulting room is upstairs." I had, she did, they accepted me.

I was 12 when Jung died.

Rejoinder by Spiegelman

I specifically thought of Dr. Fordham as a potential critic for my paper since my views are rather far from his and I believed that he would give an objective and thoughtful opinion. I was not disappointed. I thought that a second view, from someone in the younger generation of analysts, as Andrew Samuels is, would also be helpful. When he said that he thought I had a "dynamite paper" I was especially pleased, since I was under the impression that my style might be more compatible with the newer generation of analysts. Samuels, as one of the "lights" of that generation, has not disappointed me, either, and I am grateful to be understood, as he succinctly demonstrates. His story of how he came to be a Jungian is altogether delightful and much in keeping with our erratic profession. Jung only died physically when Andrew was 12–it is altogether apparent that his spirit lives on in the variety of "Jungians."

1995 Introduction to
PSYCHOTHERAPY AS A MUTUAL PROCESS
New Falcon Publications, First Edition, 1996

Many of the chapters in this book describe my developmental struggle with the phenomena of transference, which, as Jung realized even during his very first encounter with Freud, is "the alpha and omega" of analytic psychotherapy and is the testing fire for all analysts as they learn and practice their calling. And calling, I think, is the right word for his endeavor, as contrasted with craft or profession, since one needs to be "summoned" to do it by the god or gods of healing, just as the priest or shaman is "called". It is not only a joke that one hears the statement that "you have to be crazy to become an analyst" since, like the shaman, it is essential that the would-be depth therapist experience the unconscious in its fullness, which means traveling in those same realms that psychotics are forced to travel. One hopes, though, that the healer will have the added blessing of enjoying an intact and flexible ego which can, like the shaman, bring the treasure back from those same depths, rather than drown there.

I shall say more about this matter in a moment, but I want to add that there are also several chapters in this book which address analysis or therapy more generally, from the point-of-view of content, that is, what the psyche is saying in my consulting room in dreams and fantasies. All of these papers cover a thirty-year period of time and I am glad to say that I am not ashamed of any of them.

Indeed, I recognize the white heat of some, beginning with the very first one, and am glad that this heat continues to this day, more contained and alchemically transformed, but still ignited in almost each session with every analysand. Each person brings either new issues and problems or a particular slant to the collective struggle with psyche that everyone faces and, most importantly, a new and unique relationship, with me and with the unconscious, which makes this work ever fresh. It is as if the god of healing is still delighted to make his/her presence felt in the analytic transaction and it is our common task to make this conscious and transforming for both parties.

Jung noted, in his remarkable book, Psychology of the Transference, that the divine spirit, the numen, has made his/her home in the psychotherapist's consulting room. I think that Aphrodite entered into Freud's and Breuer's offices a hundred years ago, accompanying those famous hysterical women who found a powerful love there. Breuer, understandably, was scared off by what we now recognize as the phenomenon of transference, but Freud courageously–at great cost to himself–encountered her as best as he was able. Later analysts have done the same, although it took Jung to realize what was more deeply afoot. Nowadays, rules and regulations–always important as the legitimate respect for the goddess, Themis–threaten to drive Aphrodite out altogether, and it must take that powerful commitment to a therapeutic "calling" for depth therapists to continue this valuable tradition.

That leads me to comment on what I have recently recognized about my own "calling" as a healer. I am not, I think, a natural born healer. I can say this since I have had the opportunity to observe some of these naturally gifted individuals, particularly in my supervisory work. It should come as no surprise that physicians, in particular, seem to be more frequently such natally gifted healers, even though medical materialism and power drives tend to kill or distort this divine direction. But doctors are not alone in this. The healing god, like Aphrodite, comes and goes as he/she wishes and selects as its agent whomsoever it will. Those naturally "chosen" can hardly avoid it. Such folk exude compassion and natural wisdom in their pores and are ever present to healing issues. One need only teach them and go along with them on their journey to make this gift manifest. It is even often shown in early dreams of childhood. Sometimes, though, people have a calling and turn it down. I have seen this in dreams also. The god of healing seems to let some people get away with this rejection of the call and not others, who are pursued and even punished by such avoidance.

I am thinking, now, of the quite young man I saw for only a brief period not long ago. He came to me in connection with his students in a therapy training program that he was enrolled in–which required him to undergo some analysis–but he was far from believing that this was his own path. He had been deeply effected by the works of my friend, James Hillman, and had recently read his work with the theme, "We have had a hundred years of psychotherapy and the world is getting worse," in which the case is forcefully made that remaining in the confining quarters of individual self-investigation can be counter-productive when "it is the world that is sick."

My young patient was struck by the value of our work with dreams and fantasies in Jungian psychotherapy, so we found common ground with Hillman's interest in imagination. Anyway, when I sent this chap to see Hillman–as perhaps the logical person for him–the latter sent him back to me! So, we had to continue. After some interesting anima-work and an impressive dream in which he saw a statue of the Buddha come to life in a fountain, awakening a religious dimension for him in a new way, he had the following dream:

My friend, B, and I are in a reality with a history in which the South had won the Civil war. The country had been divided into the Union and the Confederacy, and the two separate nations had been completely separated. No one had been allowed to pass from one to the other since the end of the war. B. and I are in some city which borders both the Union and the Confederacy and, for the first time, people are being allowed to cross over to the Confederacy, and we go through or over something which is a cross between a bride and a tunnel. It is night in the Confederate city and the city is extremely beautiful, lit with many colored lights and exceptionally clean. It soon becomes obvious that there are no prohibitions in the Confederacy: gambling, prostitution, drugs and almost anything seems to be legal. B. and I reflect that it is for this reason that the city is so clean. Nothing is suppressed, so everything is dealt with properly. We walk through the streets of the city, admiring the feeling of excitement around, until we come across a book store. We browse the shelves for a while and we are enthralled with the variety of books. There are many books which do not exist in the Union and many of these seem to us mysterious and very intriguing.

As we walk among the shelves of books, our conversation somehow turns to metaphysical healing, that is, the healing of physical wounds or illness through mental means. B. says, "You used to be into that stuff, didn't you?" and I reply that I had, but that I had abandoned it long ago. He then pulls out a knife and stabs a fellow bookstore patron in the back of the neck and says to me, "You're a healer, now heal!" I immediately protest, "No, I don't do that anymore! I gave it up!" But my protestations are to no avail, for Bill has disappointed. I am left with this dying person, and I can find no alternative but to try and heal the person.

The wound is a vertical stab directly in the center of the back of the neck. I put my hand over it and imagine the wound closed. I remove my hand, the wound is closed for a moment, but then pops back open. I try this several more times, until finally the wound stays shut. I say to myself that is the best that I can do and leave the bookstore.

Suddenly I find myself in a somewhat large room with three large and dangerous-looking men. They tell me that they are going to kill me and that I had better defend myself. I tell them that there must be some mistake, and that I do not want to fight with them. They say that there is no mistake and begin attacking me, telling me again that they are going to kill me and that I had better defend myself.

I dodge their attacks for a while, refusing to enter the battle, but soon they have me surrounded in the center of the room. I cannot escape and I begin to fight. As the four of us struggle, for a moment we are all locked up in combat, but soon we start to turn slowly in a circle. The turning speeds up and I realize that this is no longer a battle, but a dance. Simultaneously, the room and the men are somehow transfigured, and I find myself dancing with two men and a woman in the center of a huge party. It soon becomes obvious that the party is for me and everyone is celebrating that I made it there.

This rather longish and interesting dream has many aspects, but I will only comment on a few of them. The dream begins with a statement of the dreamer's situation. It shows a changed reality. For Americans, the Civil War is a crucial symbol of the division of our country, the battle of North and South, of continuing opposition in the psyche. In the case of our dreamer, it is a battle between consciousness and the unconscious, a fundamental condition for many. Now, he is one who can "cross-over," that is can reach the unconscious and its contents. He does so, interestingly, via a bridge and a tunnel, from "above" as well as "below," which suggests that integration can take place in both ways, spirituality and instinctively. But what he finds, most unusually, is that the unconscious side, unusually experienced as the dark, repressed aspect of the soul, shows openness and freedom: everything is permitted and is therefore clean. I think that a personal level this encourages the dreamer to attend to the unconscious rather than follow his conscious bent of wanting to repair the outer world in some way. Yet I also think that the dream compensates, collectively, for this present time in our country which tends to be more legalistic, repressive and judgmental, while darkness prevails outwardly, everywhere. This is in contrast to the sixties when there was much more freedom and experimentation, particularly for youth, such as this chap.

In the unconscious he finds greater intellectual freedom and much of interest, which is very nice because this is a very bright and rebellious young man who needs to be challenged meaningfully. And here he comes upon the problem with which he came into analysis, namely, should he become a healer or not? The dream presents this as the problem of human physical wound healed by mental means, the union of mind and body, a central issue in Western consciousness for at least the last three hundred years, about which alchemy was much involved and about which Jung has written extensively.

The dreamer goes from the mental position of looking at books to the physical fact of being forced to address the problem very directly, albeit within the psychic reality of the dream. One can understand B. as his aggressive shadow who forces the action, which the dreamer tries to avoid but cannot. He succeeds, however, in the healing, after which he has to face the three dangerous men who are going to kill him. From a psychological point of view, this would suggest that when the healing issue is confronted, this brings the deeper, archetypal shadow aspect of aggression. Does the unconscious not inform us here that whoever can heal can also kill or be killed? Naturally, the opposite of this is not necessarily true. We need to recall that the great ancient physician, Hippocrates, gave all healers as the first requirement: "Only do no harm"!

Once the dreamer accepts the struggle, he now finds a masculine symbol for wholeness, a quaternity of males. So the battle take place within the masculine archetype of action, evolving into a circle, a more complete image of totality. The action now transforms into dancing, something which definitely includes the feminine element as well, shown in the fact that one of the four is a woman. Nothing less than transfiguration ensues, which clearly shows that becoming a healer is a religious issue, a spiritual issue. The celebration in his honor, I think, is that he has come home to himself, his own myth and his own "vocation." I do not know if he will indeed ultimately become a psychotherapist, but the dream seems to insist on it and, more importantly, this is in the context of healing the split between conscious and unconscious and between body and mind.

In my case, the healing path as a "vocation" emerged out of my own analytical work and was not the reason that I undertook therapy at the beginning. It may be worth telling that story for other budding therapists or analysts who may be "called" in a peculiar way, but not clearly as healers. When I began graduate school in psychology, in 1948, I planned on becoming a professor and researcher, specializing in social psychology. In one class, entitled "Critical Problems, in Psychology", the professor–the charming man but utterly committed to an exclusively behavioral view of psychology–said that he thought that one day we would have a formula for art. Without realizing that I was doing so, I blurted out, "Nonsense!" My professor did not take offense at this sign of insubordination and some discussion ensued. What I remember, though, is what happened afterwards.

I had been sitting next to an "older man" (actually in his early forties while I was all of twenty-two years old!), who commented, after class, that I had "a very interesting handwriting, musical, artistic, imaginative and original." I looked at him as if he were from another planet and asked if he did handwriting analysis. He replied that he had done so before the war, in Europe, where he had also practiced as a lawyer, but was now a Jungian analyst.

"Aren't you Jewish," I asked, to which he nodded affirmatively.

"But wasn't Jung a Nazi?" I continued, in all innocence.

"No, he was not," replied Dr. Max Zeller, for this was his name I then learned, "and I myself spent some time in a concentration camp in Germany."

Now I was really curious and asked if I might speak to him further about Jung and analysis. He graciously replied that he would do so if I wished and invited me to his home. When I asked why a Jungian analyst might be in a graduate psychology class, he replied that a colleague had suggested that he do so since a licensing law for the profession of psychotherapy was likely to be enacted soon and he was trying it out to see if it would be worthwhile for him to pursue this path. He had been accredited as a Jungian analyst in Switzerland, but without undergoing the training that traditional psychology or psychiatry provided. University psychology, it soon turned out, was not his path, and I can certainly see why this was so.

Some days later, I visited Dr. Zeller at this home and was entranced. His house was not in a wealthy area of Los Angeles, but had its own old-world charm with books, paintings, music and a gemëttlichkeit that nourished me. His family was warm and friendly as well, serving me tea and allowing us privacy for our discussion.

"How shall I tell you about Jungian psychology?" Dr. Zeller began and then answered his own question by saying, "I will tell you a dream." He then related a dream which was like a fairy tale but was also quite personal in it content. Here was food for the soul that I did not even realize that I was missing, pursuing, as I was, the rationalistic academic path. I resolved to come and have analysis with this man when I could afford to do so, just for my own development and without any idea that I might become a psychotherapist or analyst at all. After all, I had largely accepted my university's view that objective science was all that really mattered (see my dream of the sun and the flood in the chapter, "Notes from the Underground"), that clinical psychology was a bit of a scam and that Freud and Jung were largely frauds. It so happens that much in my life that I have scorned I have subsequently grown to value. I scorned Jung and became a Jungian analyst; I scorned Wilhelm Reich and underwent eight years of Reichian body work. I had contempt for chiropractors and have had many years of excellent healing at their hands, including that of my Reichian therapist, Dr. Francis Israel Regardie. So, it behooves me to suggest that one look carefully at what one scorns.

Anyway, two years later, in 1950, when I was now a teaching assistant at the University and earning some decent money, I approached Dr. Zeller and he was glad to take me on as an analysand, at fees that I could manage. That did it. By then, I had studied Rorschach and become an assistant of the world-figure in that area, Dr. Bruno Klopfer, who was also oriented in a Jungian fashion, but I still thought of myself as a social psychologist who was also learning clinical matters.

Within a year, however, all had changed. My analysis went deep rather quickly and I was totally captured by the imaginative and analytic work which revolved around relation to the unconscious. Now I wondered whether I should become a clinician or not but did not decide the issue then, getting my Ph.D. in both clinical and social psychology in 1952. Although I had already been enrolled for a year in a clinical training program, I was still undecided. I had no dreams which announced that I ought to be a healer or analyst at all!

In the meantime, there were Jungian visitors coming from Europe, largely from Zürich, to lecture in Los Angeles, such as Rivkah Kluger (then Scharf), Marie-Louise von Franz, C.A., Meier, Barbarah Hannah, plus Michael Fordham from England, all of whom impressed me mightily with their erudition, skill, charm and humor. I wanted to be among them and imagined studying at the fabulous C.G. Jung Institute in Zürich. How else to do this except by becoming an analyst? In the meantime, I had turned down an excellent academic/clinical job at a prestigious Eastern university, provided by the chairman of my doctoral committee, Dr. Franklin Fearing, wanting to continue my analysis and post-doctoral clinical training. I had also married, just before I was called into the Army at the latter part of the Korean War. I had been in the Merchant Marine for two years during World War II but the government had decided, strangely, that this was not military enough (I had sailed the world and was shot at, for heaven's sake!)–a decision which was only reversed some twenty years later–so off I went to Fitzsimmons Army Hospital in Denver, Colorado (after some weeks of basic training) to be an Army psychologist, newly married and having completed my first analysis.

It was then that I realized that my great commitment was to working with the unconscious, in whatever form it presented itself. That took precedence over being a healer. This was indeed to be my whole life's endeavor. With that insight and acceptance, my dreams now seemed to just take for granted that I would be going to Zürich one day, without any particular emphasis on healing as such. It was clear that the clear that the Self wanted me to commit myself to an ongoing relationship with the unconscious, and only then did that same Self "make use" of the analytic path as a good way to continue this work. Only much later, after my training was over in Switzerland, did the "healing God"–presenting itself with a "calling" to me–begin to manifest in my dreams and fantasies.

And this was particularly so in regard to the issue of "Mutual Process", what this book is all about. It was as if the main task was the larger spiritual path of relating to the unconscious and only after this was deeply anchored did the healing god appear and take me on somewhat original trails.

I understand all this to mean that my path was clearly in the service of the Self, as a spiritual quest, and the Self ultimately led me also into the healing art, as well as into writing and teaching. All these years since then, I have been glad of the choice and endlessly amazed and impressed at what the Self manages to do in my own life, in the life of those whom I see in analysis, and in the analytical relationship. Both the sequence of chapters on the transference and those on content of the psyche address this theme and indicate what I have learned therein.

It occurs to me that some examples of how the Self shows up as a healer in unexpected ways might be helpful to the reader. I think immediately of two examples. The first comes from the 1960s when I was, in addition to my clinical practice, on the psychology faculty of the University of California in Los Angeles. A fellow member of the department, a researcher with a behavioral perspective, honored me by referring his wife to me for some analytic work. She had a presenting dream in which a behavioral therapist was present and suggesting certain practices in re-learning. I immediately welcomed this presentation by her therapeutic animus and taught this woman the Jungian technique of "active imagination," a way of having a dialogue with the unconscious. She embraced this with alacrity and had her internal relationship with this figure who now handled the therapy, with thanks for my collaboration! After only some ten or so sessions, the therapy was completed and everyone was happy. A Jungian analyst welcomed his opposite number, a behavioral therapist, which the patient approached with a Jungian viewpoint and the work was just right. I take it that the Self, both the patient's and mine, were behind this effort and the honoring of both led to a favorable outcome. Opposites do indeed "touch" as Jung pointed out, and often positively.

Along similar lines, I am thinking of several patients of mine, who were themselves therapists, who worked with me for some time and then went on to work with other therapists, including Freudian-oriented ones. One such person became a Freudian analyst and is now a good friend of mine! Others became Jungian analysts as well, each of whom, I am proud to say, followed the Self as it manifested in their own development. Naturally, not all the people I have trained or worked with have embraced a different perspective, but I wanted to mention these as an indication that the individual "selves" of the parties can be quite different and unseen Self transcending both may well take us as far as we can go together and then help us to move on. I have had the pleasure of also doing analysis and/or supervision with Freudian, Kleinian and Reichian analysts, so that this interchange is not only a one-sided "love-affair" for me, as it is alas, for many of our Jungian colleagues, whose fascination with Object Relations is complete but whose collegial love-object does not return the interest.

The main thing, however, is that relating to a guiding "third" in the analytic relationship, whether a healing presence or the larger Self, is the modern understanding of the ancient idea of following a "calling." This conception that the Self is present as a "third" in the analytic relationship is hardly original with me. Let me here quote the famous statement of Jung (in 1929), which provides the crucial background for this realization:

> What does this demand mean (that the analyst be analyzed first)? Nothing less than the doctor is as much "in the analysis" as the patient. He is equally a part of the psychic process of treatment and therefore equally exposed to the transforming influences. Indeed, to the extent that the doctor shows himself impervious to this influence, he forfeits influence over the patient; and if he is influenced only unconsciously, there is a gap in his field of consciousness which makes it impossible for him to see the patient in true perspective. In either case the result of the treatment is compromised.

> The doctor is therefore faced with the same task which he wants his patient to face...This therapeutic demand can be clothed in a thousand different formulae, according to the doctor's beliefs. One doctor believes in overcoming infantilism, therefore he must overcome his own infantilism. Another believes in abreacting all affects–therefore he must first abreact all of his own affects. A third believes in complete consciousness, therefore he must first reach consciousness himself. The doctor must consistently strive to meet his own therapeutic demand if he wishes to ensure the right sort of influence over his patients. All these guiding principles of therapy make so many ethical demands, which can be summed up in the single truth: be the man through whom you wish to influence others. Mere talk has always been counted hollow, and there is no trick, however artful, by which this simple truth can be evaded in the long run...the fact of being convinced and not the thing we are convinced of–that is what has always, and at all times, worked. (Jung, 1929, Coll. Wks. Vol. 16, "Problems of Modern Psychology", ¶166-7)

This potent statement of Jung provided, early on, an accurate observation of what the analytic relationship consists in and was further spelled out in depth in his great book on the transference (Coll. Wks. Vol. 16, "Psychology of the Transference"), written in 1946, which made use of the images from the medieval alchemical text, the Rosarium Philosophorum. It has taken many years and many analysts' efforts, from all schools, to work out the "implications" of these facts. The early psychoanalytic attitude of "maintaining objectivity" and trying to stay apart from these effects gave way to the realization by Melanie Klein and the subsequent Object Relations analysts, such as Bion, Winnicott, etc., that the analytic process did indeed draw the analyst fully into the psyche of the patient. They dealt with this fact by using the concept of projective identification, of the patient "putting into" the analyst those aspects of himself/herself which were troublesome or pathological, etc. This process is either conscious or unconscious and is surely present at times. But, as I spell out (together with the astrophysicist V. Mansfield, in the 1995 paper, "On the Physics and Psychology of the Transference as an Interactive Field"), this causal perspective must also give way, at deeper levels, to an acausal, synchronistic, "mutual process" perspective in which the archetypal content is constellated by the relationship itself. But I shall leave the reader to see how this is arrived at and developed over the course of the years. Suffice it to say that the archetypal perspective, which Jung discovered, shows us that the Self is both the guiding force in the work and is that which is worked on, requiring, ultimately, "mutual process."

I think that the community is now more ready to embrace this idea of mutuality than it was thirty years ago, when I wrote my first paper, or even ten years ago. The Logos position of needing to separate from the analysand and teach him/her to relate to the unconscious via active imagination and other solitary tasks (in the classical Jungian perspective), or to maintain separateness and objectivity and reveal nothing of the analyst's inner workings (in the classical Freudian perspective) has been either augmented (in the Jungian view) or displaced by the Eros position of focus on the relationship itself.

My understanding of this change is enhanced by the realization that the continuing manifestation of the feminine aspect of the Self in collective consciousness (announced in Jung's "Answer to Job" in 1952), is showing itself in the therapeutic field by greater focus on the relationship and on the body. The Goddess is friendly to these aspects and to mutual process, in my experience. And so the climate, now, is better than it was some time ago (see the chapter on The Image of the Jungian Analyst and the Problem of Authority) to consider these things. I recall showing a copy of the first two paper in this book, many years ago, to a respected, senior Jungian analyst who then proceeded to go through them and mark the items "true" or "false"! I realized that he did not have a clue about what I was dealing with, despite his erudition and deep Jungian commitment. I hope that I will not, in turn, be so blind to the next generation's discoveries or experiences.

So, here is the record of the investigation, the ideas and examples. Some of these papers have been published in various journals, and some in abstruse publications, or not at all. The record of publication and translation can be found in the Appendix. It is indeed a bit wry that some of these papers have appeared in Japanese without having been printed in English! A couple have also been translated into Italian. Like my Zürich teacher, C.A. Meier, my work has been more popular with Japanese and Italians, why I can not say. Yet my dreams, years ago, did announce this fact. Long, long ago, I dreamt that I was talking with C.G. Jung intently when he was called away to have serious discussions with the Pope. In the meantime, I was to do analysis with an Italian artist/poet who needed healing for a wounded heart. And my last dream upon finishing training in Zürich in 1959 (see the chapter on Robert to Alma Mater), announced my being open to the "Land of the Rising Sun", following which, in reality, I enjoyed the opportunity of working with several analysands from Japan when I returned to Los Angeles. So, the Self seems to know the future as well as the past, sometimes giving us glimpse of it in dreams and visions.

It has been my task and good fortune to continue in the spirit of Jung and to advance our understanding of the mutual effort of analyst and analysand and to see how the archetypes manifest in that relationship an dhow, particularly, the larger Self has chosen our own little therapeutic rooms to appear as a numen. In conclusion, I find that I can do nothing better than quote the final two paragraphs of Jung's discussion of the second picture of the Rosarium, where he cogently places this work in psychological and historical context (Vol. 16, ¶448-9):

> Individuation has two principal aspects: in the first place it is an internal and subjective process of integration, and in the second it is an equally indispensable process of objective relationship. Neither can exist without the other, although sometimes the one

and sometimes the other predominates. This double aspect has two corresponding dangers. The first is the danger of the patients's using the opportunities for spiritual development arising out of the analysis of the unconscious as a pretext for evading the deeper human responsibilities, and for affecting a certain spirituality" which cannot stand up to moral criticism; the second is the danger that atavistic tendencies may gain ascendancy and drag the relationship down to a primitive level. Between this Scylla and that Charybdis there is a narrow passage, and both medieval Christian mysticism and alchemy have contributed much to its discovery.

Looked at in this light, the bond established by the transference–however hard to bear and unintelligible it may seem–is vitally important not only for the individual but also for society, and indeed for the moral and spiritual progress of mankind. So, when the psychotherapist has to struggle with difficult transference problems, he can at least take comfort in these reflections. He is not just working for this particular patient, who may be quite insignificant, but for himself as well and his own soul, and in so doing he is perhaps laying an infinitesimal grain in the scales of humanity's soul. Small and invisible as this contribution may be, it is yet an opus magnum for it is accomplished in a sphere by lately visited by the numen, where the whole weight of humankind's problems have settled. The ultimate questions of psychotherapy are not a private matter–they represent a supreme responsibility.

NOTES FROM THE UNDERGROUND - A VIEW OF LOVE AND RELIGION FROM A PSYCHOTHERAPIST'S CAVE (1969)

A chapter from *Psychotherapy as a Mutual Process*
New Falcon Publications, First Edition, 1996

I think of my consulting room as a cave–a place where people retreat from the light of the sun and come to gaze at the dark world of their psyches, that place of dreams, fantasies, secrets, worries, desires, fears. After eighteen years as a psychotherapist, ten as a Jungian analyst in private practice, I think of myself as a groundhog in that cave and, therefore, these notes come from Underground. I am surfacing now, after years in the darkness below, to see whether it is safe to come out. I am afraid that the nuggets of dreams and visions which I have been privileged to observe will not be received, or will be seen as fool's gold rather than the real thing. The groundhog is said to be sensitive to shadow–should it cover him as he emerges, he goes back into the ground.

Before I speak about the gold, a word about the place of the psychotherapist in a discussion of love and religion. What can he say about these huge issues which has not already been said? Before Freud, the issues of love were left to poets; and before Jung, religion was the province of theologians. After these two giants of psychology had reported their observations of the soul from the viewpoint of their own caves, the situation changed. The revolution of depth psychology in the twentieth century had shaken and removed the old institutional authorities, substituting itself briefly as an all-knowing, scientific priesthood. But now we are at a time when most modern men find no one particularly authoritative in either love or religion.

For the most part, the Freudians and Jungians, revolutionary in their day, have become part of the Establishment; the young gravitate to them less and less. I have yet to hear positive words from my older colleagues about contemporary youth's ways of love and worship. For them it is "dissociated group-sexuality" and "doped-consciousness religion." Nor are the young less negative about their elder's "hypocritical morality" and "loveless lives."

So, as there are no experts, I shall speak of the psyche as show to me over the past years in dreams, fantasies and problems of my patients–and myself. Together with the demise of the expert there is a death of that shaky belief in a thing called pure objectivity. We are all creatures of psyche, as well as of our time, we all speak out of our own condition; we all speak ultimately about ourselves. Therefore, it is incumbent upon us to acknowledge that subjectivity and to speak from it and about it when we address ourselves to such important matters as love and religion.

Patients complain of too little love, giving and getting. So, by love I mean the need for emotional closeness, for sexual gratification, for relationship–fundamentally, the need for union at various levels: spirit, body, soul. Patients suffer from problems of religion: the need for meaning, for answers concerning who one is, why one is here, what it is all about, where is the numinous and awesome, is there a God, and what is He like?

Because of their reflective and soul-searching needs, people who are forced to "tune in" on their psyches and become aware not only of the spirit of the time, but also experience and intuit that which others in the culture tend to discover only after. Freud's interest in sexuality, for example, despite the academic outcry at the time, reflected only that which was going on in the unconscious of Western civilization. He anticipated long in advance and helped create a new attitude toward love and sexuality. The same holds true for Jung in the religious field. We are still a long way from grasping all these giants discovered. Although with the help of our introspection and soul-searching, I believe we may approach this immense task, and glimpse aspects of the future.

Let me give an example from one of my dreams. Eighteen years ago, when I was studying psychology in graduate school and was already in analysis, I dreamed:

> I was walking on campus on a bright, clear day. Many others were strolling, too. Suddenly, there arose from the sea a tidal wave which swept toward the campus. Other people were distraught, and ran in anguish. I was fascinated by the sea, particularly by the white caps and foam of the waves. Finally, the sea began to inundate the campus, and I climbed the scaffolding of a building that was just being constructed. I was uncertain if this scaffolding would protect me from the tidal wave. The feeling was, however, that once the water had flooded the campus and receded, this would a new and better place than before.

The dream speaks of my situation: it hints at the impending end of my days as a student, as well as an end, as a consequence of analysis, of those clear-skied, rationalistic, academic attitudes with which I had been trained. But the dream also portrays a larger than personal event. The unconscious in its collective form as the ocean invades the institutional area of light, of rational consciousness. I am fascinated by the unconscious, particularly in its foaming, eros aspect. Aphrodite was foam-born, you recall. The wave sweeps the campus and I finally climb a new structure that might survive the invasion. The lysis or end of the dream is uncertain, but there is hope for a new consciousness to emerge, on which will survive the seeping away of the detritus of the old rationality, perhaps. The wave may fertilize like the inundations of the Nile; it may be occasion for a rebirth of a feminine, eros aspect.

All this was certainly true of my personal psyche at the time and mirrors accurately what place in my development for some years afterwards. But the dream also speaks of a collective level, of a campus, of an institution, of a flood, all greatly beyond my personal concerns.

As I see it, the dream anticipated the flood that subsequently hit many college campuses. To me it is not too fantastic to think that the tidal wave of passion and love which I glimpsed at that time, in the relative safety of analysis, slumbered also in the souls of my contemporaries. Since that time, the flood of revolution has increasingly swept the campuses. I am inclined to believe that the dream had objective significance and that its lysis is going on right now. It is an open question whether there will be a new attitude on the campuses, a place where the feminine principle will also reign. Is not the emphasis of the students upon love, and beauty, upon emotion, and nature? That flooding took me far from the University, and eventually brought me to my own cave.

What is it that I have found in my careful attention to the psyche? (That, by the way, is another and valuable definition of religion: the "careful attention" to the numinous, to that tremendum which fascinates us and frightens us, wherever it occurs. My own piety may be, indeed, a religion of the psyche). I have found that the old images of God have died or fast dying–hence the "God is dead" ideology. This means that the authority, creativity, power for good and evil which was previously experienced or projected upon a "God out there" is no longer viable, and that God has taken up residence in the human soul. Thus we are fascinated with the psyche. But this God who dwells in the psyche is not so readily apparent. He makes Himself known first in the images and forms of the past, e.g., Greek, Jewish, Christian. More-over, these psychic parts war in ways which are astonishing. Freud saw this already as the battle between the superego–a judging and punishing Jehovah–and the id, a daimonic child who seeks pleasure amid the breakage of all rules. Jung saw this—more accurately, I think—as the mythological play of archetypal images, man living out a myth unawares.

Jung saw that the God-image in some men pushed them towards realizing the "God-within." This he called Individuation—that process of struggle between nature and nurture, the given and the possible, a road which winds a long way, resulting in uniqueness. The symbols which emerge on such a path, the exciting, miraculous, and painful steps of so profound and often lonely a journey, are graphically described in the example of Jung through his autobiography, *Memories, Dreams, Reflections*.

Jung thought the process of Individuation was aristocratic, limited to the few. In the years since I have been watching this in myself and others, however, I found that Individuation is much more common than Jung believed. Indeed, I have found that many—most, even—of those people in analysis for more than a year have been fundamentally gripped or plagued by this process. The evidence comes from their dream symbols, their interminable struggles that, on the surface, should be readily reconcilable.

The slang for Individuation might well be "doing your own thing," which, of course, many people now embrace. And there is a strong sanction to take this path. But to do one's own thing as a conscious process, to follow the course of one's uniqueness and creativity, to branch out and away from established patterns, be they of family, country, profession or religion, really to Do One's Own Thing, is very difficult and painful. Nevertheless, I think that the conscious taking up of one's psychic development is increasing and partly accounts for the breakdown of outer authority and old standards.

What, then, of the previously accepted images of God "among us"? Rejection does not sweep them away. The abandoned Gods of the fathers continue to exist in oneself as autonomous devils or take up residence in the many "isms" which abide in the world.

Communism, Scientism, Psychologism, Drugism are just a few of the dead Gods of Judaism, Christianity, Greek Paganism that have survived in other forms. The compensatory and evolutionary nature of the psyche, however, suggest that new, collective images of God would appear. Also, man's social nature requires a new image of the Divine.

Will this new image be another variation of the Christian myth? I think it will; for the image of God in a particular culture rises naturally out of antecedents. The next development in Western man may well take its source from the religion which has been dominant for two thousand years, Christianity. Even if the Christian religion "dies," its seeds could take an underground path of growth so that the new myth will continue certain Christian features. Let me illustrate this direction from a dream of a non-Christian man who, all the same, had to struggle internally with Christian symbolism:

> I am standing on a hill overlooking a valley. Just beyond the valley is another hill, as high as the one I am on. The region is semi-arid and dry, but has the atmosphere of a beautiful desert region in either New Mexico or Israel. Many people are gathered on both hills, walking about expectantly. There is tenseness and electricity in the air. Far down the valley, and upwards towards some high mountains, there is a small group of people. They walk together, seemingly following one man. As they come closer, one can see a certain radiance around the heads of all these people. I am startled to see that these must be halos. It is a light, a glow about them. I feel glad, as if I understand something by experiencing, by seeing, that which had been puzzling to me.
>
> As they come closer, I see that the man in the lead is Christ, but he is nothing like the pictures I have seen. He is tall and dark and quite muscular. He even resembles the movie-actor Charlton Heston. He walk firmly, even angrily. Nothing is said, but as they come close to us and directly before us in the valley below, all of us, on both hills, know that Christ is returning and that he is

returning angrily. His anger is because he has been misrepresented and he is now returning to the world to change all that.

The Christ of this dream is far, indeed, from those sentimental paintings popular during the last centuries. I think of Philip Roth's novel, *Portnoy's Complaint*, in which the Jewish hero recalls these pale pictures in a Catholic home; he wonders how Christians can conceive as God what Portnoy considers "The Pansy of Palestine." The Christ of the dream is as angry as the one who drove out the money-changers; he is also muscular, strong, and handsome—even if still slightly tainted by sentimentality, now in Hollywood colors. But this Christ has body! That seems the great change of the new aeon: the God of Love can have a Body. Perhaps this new God of Love will even make love as well as preach it.

In contrast, I would like to show another aspect of the changing Christian myth. This time the dreamer is a young woman in her early twenties. She has come for therapy because after having given birth to a child out of wedlock, she suffered from anxiety and bodily vibrations which made her feel as if she were going to die. What emerged in the analysis was not that she had unconscious guild about having a bastard child; rather, that she had been deprived by her modern, very competent physician from experiencing the actual birth of her baby. She had been knocked out and had the baby taken from her both in the birth process and afterwards. She needed to have that natural experience, not to be treated like some freak, object, or "fallen woman." The young woman dreamed as follows (the boy-friend of the dream, incidentally, is not the father of the child but a current relationship):

> My boy-friend and I are in bed together, making love, but having some trouble. At that moment, Jesus comes into the room, stark naked, and announces that this is "The Age of Immaculate Conception."

The dreamer was raised agnostically in an enlightened, formerly Christian household. The dreamer enjoyed sex and had no apparent "hung-up" with it. She also was in a reasonably good relationship with her boy-friend. The meaning that emerged from our work was that Jesus was speaking about the need to have a God within. She was being pressed to give birth, within herself, to a God-man. Not only she, the dreamer, was so pressed, but what is emerging Jesus says, is a whole "Age of Immaculate Conception." Men and the new God-image can be born in a state of grace, not through "sin." This has a very deep and far-reaching implication; nothing less than the redemption of men; or as the Bible anticipates, when all men will "be as Gods."

Lest you think this is a sweet story that causes the dreamer no pain, let me assure you that the coming-to-be of the Christ image is fare from pleasant, edifying, or marvelous. Mostly it is hell. For it means crucifixion, an inner torness between opposites of desire versus duty, of morality versus love, or even of one duty against another, one love against another. Such people do perform an imitatio Christi, but they do so not out of a wish nor because they are Christians, for such a God-image occurs among Jews, Christians, Agnostics, and even Buddhists! It is a syncretic thing that is happening.

Let me give you an example from the dream of a woman who was born Jewish and given a Catholic education, subsequently to become, like moderns of her day, agnostic. This woman dreamt that she saw Christ upon the cross, but that he was dead, or nearly dead. She then began to make oral love to him, fellatio. The Christ stirred and gradually came to life. He then descended from the cross and, despite the dreamer's desire that he remain with her, went off "about his father's business," although he was much appreciative of her love. Her dream ended at that point, but the subsequent experience of her life, of being torn apart in loving a man, in trying to be true to her love at the cost of her security, her family, her reputation, showed how she experienced the "coming to life" of the God of love within her. She drank deeply of this spirit and was often abandoned by it. She had many agonies until a feminine Self could be born which could encompass this great spirit of love.

You will note the rather uncanonical presentation of Jesus being loved orally. Such things do happen in dream and fantasy. This imagery is not so far afield even within the tradition of the Church. In the sacrament of the Mass, the God is incorporated; he is eaten, body and blood. This deep cannibalism of the soul is one of the most profound expressions of the idea that one assimilates, takes in, integrates a particular psychological or experiential content. However, the oral love of the dream is a taking in, a loving which his not cannibalistic. It takes up that which Victorians thought of as pathological cannibalistic. It takes up that which Victorians thought of as pathological and even Freud considered "infantile," and makes such love holy, special and profound, not pathological.

The dream of this woman is not unique. A comparable series of dreams from one man shows a similar development. Furthermore, these dreams indicate that the archetypal background for the God of love does not restrict itself to Christian symbolism and dogma alone. The man dreamt that a dark and powerful, demonic figure was going to teach women to love by first compelling fellatio and then requiring that the women lick up the remains of the semen. This was followed by a vivid illustration with various women. The dreamer awakened with sexual desire, fear, and disgust. He was confronted with a dark Eros, a "mighty daimon," as Plato tells us. Some time later, this same man dreamt of a peculiar priest-wizard who had a number of women around him, all of whom were being instructed in the ways of love-making as a religious rite. Again, the main ritual for such expression lay in oral love. Still later, the man dreamt that a 'Redeemer had been born of a sweet, but passionate young woman, unknown, yet one that the dreamer had been intimate with. The dream father, however, was both "unknown" yet related to this same demonic God hovering in the background.

I believe the unconscious picks such "polymorphous perverse" sexual symbolism in the portrayal of its new God images, because the psyche is trying to restore and re-divinize those aspects of bodily love which have been rejected as taboo. This was anticipated by D. H. Lawrence. In *The Man Who Died* Lawrence beautifully describes the experience of the man, Jesus, going from the crucifixion to a priestess in Egypt, who teaches him love in the flesh. In a similar vein is *The Holy Sinner* by Thomas Mann and some of the works of Henry Miller. However, in our time, where has sex has become almost blasé, it is no longer the opening up or even the valuing of sexuality which can shock us, rather the new shocking thing for our western consciousness is the re-divinization of sexuality. That God can have a penis as well as an all-seeing eye! That God can make love as well as preach about it!

I think these are hints of the new God-image. He is a demon and from the Underworld, but he is not the devil, nor even a devil. The devil of Christian tradition is an unavoidable negative brother to the all-positive Jesus-image of God. The emerging image is different. He is demonic as passion and love and sexuality can be demonic, with their aspects of jealousy rage, possessiveness, desire. This demon is from the Underworld in that he is a spirit which dwells in the flesh, emerges from the flesh as in the spiraling upwards of the serpent-like energies of the autonomic nervous system in Kundalini Yoga. But he is also romantic and gentle.

Some years ago, I dreamed:

> I had been on a long journey and had come to a place in the Underworld. I entered a room which was much like a cave. This cave was dark, but I could see on the wall a very beautiful tapestry which seemed to have its own sources of light from within itself The tapestry looked something like those pictures of Columbus discovering the New World, but this was a Knight-Soldier-Discoverer, accompanied by an American Indian, stepping ashore under a bright sun. But what they were finding ashore was a figure which looked like the alchemical Mercurius, a hermaphroditic being with golden light about him. I was impressed by this beautiful tapestry but then became aware that in this room was living figure, large and awesome. I came closer and found a dark, powerful man, chained to the floor by means of a circular handcuff. An unknown source made me aware that this figure was a God-man and related to the Mercurius of the tapestry. I had in my own pocket the key that would unlock the chains and free him. The choice was mine. I hesitated for a moment as to whether to free such an unknown and powerful being, and then did so. At the next moment, this being and I were going at great speed, like arrows, the dream suggested, towards the City. At the same moment, I was aware that the God-man was himself like an arrow.

The God-man of the dream seemed to me none other than Eros, the mighty demon of love who had been rejected by Christianity and gone underground. This God of Love was somehow related to Mercurius, about which Jung has written so much, and which involves the chief labor in the alchemical work in the individuation process. Further, there is a hint of another sort of discover, similar in kind to that of Columbus of the New World, but this time the Indian is accompanying Columbus! I concluded that the realization of this tapestry, the work of art, devotion and love, is to bring back to the city, to society, to life, the demon Eros, the love-God.

The subsequent course of my life has, indeed, involved such struggles, realizations, dismemberments and crucifixions as difficult and trying as those of my patients. My understanding of what has resulted over the years of coping with these demon Eros, this archetypal representative of aspects of the self which have been overlooked in our culture, is that this God wants to become Man, just as Jung hypothesized. It is as if the living of these conflicts both humanizes the God-image and divinizes man. We have had God the Father, God the Son, and now God the Holy Spirit has descended into Everyman and is becoming God the Brother. God becomes more human and men become more God-like when they take up this dismembering struggle to allow God to live in their own souls rather than to project him elsewhere.

Along with the new image of God, there seems to be emerging an image of a Goddess. Because the old image of God is dead, the psyche seems now to be bringing up repressed and ignored aspects of the soul. Among these discarded parts of the psyche, much will be feminine, as would be expected from depth psychological theory. We have evidence also from our culture in the recent enhancement of what have been thought of as feminine values: feeling, intuition, body, the personal, the irrational, beauty–in contrast to their masculine opposites of thought, fact, spirit, the impersonal, the rational, utility. To shed some light upon what historical transformations these changes are alluding to, let me begin by telling a dream.

This dream is from a woman who is herself a practicing psychotherapist, has had many years of analysis with various analysts, is Jungian in her orientation. I mention the Jungian orientation for several reasons. First, Jung plays an important role in the dream. Second, among modern psychologists, Jung has been most aware of the feminine principle in the psyche and has gone further systematically to include and accept this aspect.

The dreamer is informed by Jung that he can see her if she wishes. She has been having an analytic hour with an old woman analyst, a trusted friend as well, and now prepares the room for Jung. She is competent and at home in it, but has difficulty lighting the fire. She finally does so as Jung comes in. She laughs, but feels exasperated. Jung mimic her and she feels that he is picking up something deep within her she wants to get at. She is aware of being connected with ancient women, Babylonians. The deep ironical laughter has something to do with the Whore of Babylon.

Jung and the dreamer sit close together, and Jung asks if the dreamer has thought about what is behind the archetypes. The dreamer starts to respond from knowledge in a previous dream and Jung is delighted and comes close. He then speaks of a grandson, but not his biological one. After that, Jung complains of pain, seems to grow old and rigid, his hands blacken and fall away. It is a shock and horrible to the dreamer. Jung is matter of fact and dispassionate about it. He has lived long enough, but can't tell how long it will be before he will die.

This is a long and complicated dream, but I will relate some of what we both concluded as to the dream's meaning. She has a deeply feminine, ancient thing within her which "Jung" can pick up, but which can not yet be expressed. It has to do with Babylon and the Whore. I shall come back to this symbol later. "Jung" then asks her about what is beyond his own theory and the dreamer has some ideas, males, his grandson. Finally, he grows hardened, rigid, and ready for death. Jungian psychology in general could be reflected in this dream as having become unfortunately rigid, and just because of this inability to get access to the deep and ancient feminine principle which wants to express itself. It seems to take several generations, according to "Jung" in this dream, for such an assimilations. I think that this is true. Very few of the colleagues of my generation, Jung's "grandsons," so to speak, have been compelled to take up this challenge of the ancient feminine. The dreamer herself, however, has already done considerable work in this area and, I believe, it will be women who will be carrying the expression, the coming into being, of the ancient, neglected feminine aspect.

What is this aspect? The qualities of the Goddess which are being reawakened can be subsumed under the name, Witch. The Witch, this dark and magical principle, ancestress of the matriarchal religions, this threat to the austere disciple of Protestant Christianity, to the monotheism of Judaism and to the rationality of science, brings with it the occult, such as astrology and magic and darkly sensual, such as is recalled when we think of the Whore of Babylon.

This Witch figures appears in dreams in many guises. When negative, she can be like Mrs. Portnoy in the book by Roth I mentioned earlier–unloving, unconscious, negatively self-involved, hostile, bitchy. She can also, in her deeper aspects, drive a person crazy. I have seen many people, including myself, in witch-states of enormous pain and frustration. These are the negative emotions of love: jealousy, hatred, envy, rage. There is the negative feeling of frustrated life: feeling impotent, unable to act, torn apart. There is the pathology of fear and distrust–suspicion all the way to paranoia, twisting of reality, feeling, often rightly, that one is a victim. There is also the darkening of consciousness which blots out memory of anything good.

Such is the experience of one who is caught in a witch-complex, in the negative feminine of the emerging dark Goddess. One terrible aspect of the witch-complex is the inability to express in words. Remember what happened to the Babylonians? Their tower of Babel, their multiform modes of expression, along with attempt to reach Heaven itself, was struck down by the patriarchal God. And Babylon, including the Goddess, was left speechless. She is beginning to return, but is having trouble expressing herself.

The agnostic woman I mentioned earlier, who took on the oral love of Christ, dreamt that she saw the witch suffering terrible agony in hell. But she was unable to utter a sound, and one could sense her agony only from her eyes and face. This inability to say what is happening occurs commonly. Sometimes the words are not available; sometimes the words would hurt too much if they came out. Sometimes one must not speak or cannot. This is a hell of dismemberment.

Just as the male Eros-God has in his Christian form an aspect of pain and horror, symbolized by the suspension between the opposites in the Crucifixion, the female Witch-Goddess has the symbol of being roasted in the fire when she is alone with the agony of her state, and the symbol of dismemberment. The breaking up of one's psyche into pieces is horrible. I recall a dream of my own of this kind. I saw the mother of an old friend of mine, dark and dreary, with flat, suffering eyes. She seemed to be accusing me of something; I was guilty. I awakened feeling depressed, lifeless, worried and full of obsessive rumination–just as the woman used to be, and vaguely guilty. That was a witch state. And her flat suffering eyes were mine: I had lost all vision, all perspective of my situation. This loss of reality is a feeling of dismemberment.

I have mentioned only the negative of this Goddess. What of the positive? This might be seen as an image of a new feminine Self–a beautiful and passionate Gypsy, for example: a woman of spirit who can also love and be independent. I recall a dream of a woman who had worked hard in analysis for several years:

> She had been on a long sea voyage with many people, all those whom she loved, cared for, was involved with, including her analyst. At one point, she knew that she would have to leave all these people in order to find herself. She chose to accept this fate, despite the pain, and leaped over the side of the ship, sinking down into the depths of the sea. After having difficulty

breathing, she finally saw a beautiful golden flower, growing from the depths of the ocean, and that gave her peace, serenity, and primarily, a deep acceptance of herself as unique, an individual different from all others.

This dream shows the aspect of the witch which compels the woman to go against eros, love, and relationship, and to be alone. She has to be alone to find her spirit and also to come to her deepest feminine self, the biological plant level of the flower. The dreamer did not know of the symbolism of the oriental golden flower, about which Jung has written a commentary, but she experienced in her soul that profound union of male and female, yang and yin, which brought her the serenity of self-acceptance. Later on she dreamt that she was being hounded on all sides by the people she loved and who loved her; she could handle it only by feeling, just at her back, this same golden flower. Thus does the feminine self, this mandala of tender wholeness show itself.

There are many dreams from women which show that they must travel the road of their individuation via love. And their love will be painful, unconventional. Emotion, passion, irrational intuition must all be included. The witch is bringing back a darkly feminine love of deep personal involvement, of the endurance of pain and the dismemberment of being unable to take action. It is the love of Aphrodite in all its forms, sensual, dark, full of intensity.

This also means taking one's opposite in many ways. Here, I am reminded of a woman who could always love, tenderly and passionately, but who had difficulty expressing herself verbally. After a painful period of struggle such as I have described, there emerged in her, almost perfectly, whole poems of love. This woman had never had training in writing of any kind, but the level of struggle produced an expression of deeply beautiful and philosophical poems, expressing primarily the paradoxes of love. We see, thus, that the witch, with her phallic nose and aerial broom, is also united with a maleness, a being which expresses itself in spirit.

The lack of communication in words also suggests the feminine need for non-verbal expression, for touch and taste and smell, as well as talk. She is there, is she not, in the current sensory awareness laboratories?

The archetype of the witch is also bringing forth a new form of consciousness—a new Logos, as well as a new Eros. This new form of consciousness is quite different from that having prevailed for many hundreds of years. It is personal rather than impersonal, concrete rather than scientific, irrational rather than rational. Even though feminine and different from the prevailing consciousness, it is yet consciousness. It is already found in fields such as the healing arts, which combine science and art, require intuition and the personal touch. Psychotherapy itself is just such a field.

This old-new consciousness is associated with the occult, with astrology, Tarot, and all kinds of divination—with what has been called the Black Arts. They are coming back, despite being driven out by science. And now, hopefully, there is enough of the scientific consciousness and reason among all of us to be able to look at, to reintegrate that which has been rejected and repressed. From where I sit in my cave, the popularity of astrology, of all the occult books, of Eastern ways of religion, of meditation, and the like, as an awakening of the feminine, of the mother as opposed to the father, of the sister as opposed to the brother, of the mother-daughter myth as opposed to the father-son myth of Oedipus. All these are ways of saying that a new kind of consciousness is being born. But this new feminine God-image is not yet fully clear, partly because, being feminine, she never will be "clear" the way our rational, scientific, blue-skied consciousness would like. But partly, too, because her outlines are not fully apparent but are developing along with us. In short, I think that God the Sister is emerging along with God the Brother, and that we all, men and women, are partners in helping to realize this event. That is what is meant to me by the hermaphroditic character of the Mercurius in my dream and in alchemy. I think, too, that this is what the process of individuation is about: for each of us to realize in our souls and in our loves an emerging and self-realizing He-She God. For is not the totality a union of equals, of male and female, of yang and yin, of father and mother and also, in the coming time, of brother and sister, as the alchemical imagery puts it?

I have portrayed this event in a book of mythical-psychological tales which tells about ten people of different religions who meet in Paradise. After they have pursued their individuation processes, they find communality in the experience of the God-Goddess becoming manifest within them. My ow psyche resonates particularly with that aspect of Jewish mysticism called Kabbalah. The Tree of the Sephiroth, with it's imagery of male and female unions of various kinds, is a tenfold image of God. This goes beyond the Trinity in its apparent polytheism, but it still holds the oneness, the monotheism, for those ten aspects of are but the faces of the One God. Also, the Kabbalah image of the wedding of God with his own feminine Shekhina, which lies in the soul of man and must be realized on earth in the community of humankind, suits me psychologically very well.

Much more could and needs to be said about this emerging consciousness of feminine Logos and masculine Eros. I am aware that I have not differentiated two from each other sufficiently and that I have only sketched their portraits in outline. But time requires that I leave it at that now. I mean both the time permitted for the presentation tonight and also this time in history, when we are touched with only glimpses, with hints, with intuitions of the future and discern only outlines.

Introduction to
JUNGIAN PSYCHOLOGY AND THE PASSIONS OF THE SOUL
New Falcon Publications, First Edition, 1989

Who has not struggled with the passions of the soul? It seems to be our human condition to be endlessly tossed about on the seas of desire, guarding our little crafts of free will with restraint lest we tumble and drown, losing our feeble lights of consciousness. Self-help books of all kinds instruct us in ways to tame our anger, guide our fantasies toward achieving those sought-after, sometimes unattainable, objects and ideals which we hope will satisfy us. Even if we are fairly calm ourselves, our venturing on the freeways of life exposes us to violence and disregard, to other people's passions, which can also toss us into that sea, either by emotional contagion or by impact.

Yet even without the toxic thrust of crowded, modern city life, we are confronted from within. Images and fantasies arise; they also move us out of our calm or out of our routine condition and propel us into questionable action or more fantasy. We unconsciously dialogue with ourselves and try to control these passions in some meaningful way.

But our passions are not only dark and disruptive. They are joyful and ecstatic, pleasurable and fulfilling, sometimes with "objects"–as psychoanalese puts it–sometimes just with the emotions themselves. We are surely seekers after pleasure, as Freud understood, but we are also more than that. We are also driven by the urge to power, as Adler comprehended, but above all, as Jung recognized, we are creatures who require meaning in our lives. Without meaning and purpose, without connection to a higher principle which gives us direction and significance, we also drown, this time in a sea of meaninglessness and chaos.

Nor are our passions so clear-cut and distinctive. We all seek happiness, to be sure, but it is not so easily defined. Among the happiest periods of my life was during the latter half of the 1950s when my wife and I lived in Zürich, Switzerland. At long last, I had the chance to study at the C.G. Jung Institute, to undergo analysis again, and to train, along with fellow seekers from all over the world, in the profession I had chosen. My analytic work was far from smooth; it was filled, as it should be, with passions of all kinds. Yet, despite the depressions, despite the frustrations, I was happy as I could be. Why? I could focus on the soul and my life was filled with meaning. I felt that I was at the Omphallos, as the Greeks put, the Navel of the World. When one is focussed on the Self, the central core of one's being, one is centered not only at one's own navel, so to speak, but truly at the Navel of the World, allied with the deepest aspects of the souls of us all. To be immersed both in my inner world and in the outer world of European tradition and culture was to be at once rooted and searching. To share this search and longing with Egyptians, Swedes, Frenchmen, Germans, British, Americans, etc. was to sense, at last, the great Self of us all. That was the gift of Jung to so many of us, and that was the special boon that some of us could suffer/enjoy in those last years when his spirit and that of his immediate followers could find a valued place in the scheme of things.

Jung's psychology was not popular then. It was a period, prior to the storm of the 60s, when life–in America, at least–was relatively safe, conventional, ordered, and rather materialistic. It was wonderful to find, at the Institute, like-minded people from everywhere, east and west, who felt engaged in a similar spiritual search. Our present day is even more materialistic–and now this view prevails in much of the world–so we are once again in need of that Paradise where inner meaning and outer structure are in some harmony. Whenever that condition prevails, fragmentation is overcome and we experience happiness and fulfillment.

But most of us experience these periods of happiness and fulfillment in a limited way: sometimes for months or years, sometimes for moments only, sometimes never. Heaven is often on earth, but certainly not more often than Hell. Indeed, most of us experience the various stages of Purgatory much of the time. And this purgatory is the condition of our struggle with our passions.

The shorter Oxford English Dictionary informs us that the word, "passion," from the original Latin, *passionem*, means "suffering." It further gives three senses in which "passion" can be understood: (1) the suffering of pain, as with some bodily affliction, or the Passion of Jesus Christ (spelled with a capital P); (2) being passive, or affected by outside forces; (3) an affection of the mind: any vehement, commanding, or overpowering emotion; in psychology and art, any mode in which the mind is affected or acted upon, as ambition, avarice, desire, hope, fear, love, hatred, joy, grief, anger, revenge. The latter two uses also arise from the Greek, *pathos*, which also means emotion or deep feeling. And, from these comes our word "patient," one who bears pain, enduring and long-suffering.

So, from these definitions it is surely right for a psychotherapist and Jungian analyst to write about the "passions of the soul," since that is our daily bread, so to speak, that which we chew upon and digest, together with our patients. We hope to transform and be transformed by the passions which arise in the work, coming from within and from without, afflict the soul and make our lives different from animals.

It is there, perhaps, where we need to begin: animals do not suffer the passions as we do. They are God's loyal creatures, doing exactly what they are supposed to do, following the instinctive paths laid down for them. They are not required to suffer the crucifixion of opposites such as morality versus desire, lust versus love, ambition versus kindness. And that is why the juxtapositions of the above definitions of passion, active and passive, is strange from a definitional point of view, but so true psychologically.

But I must correct what I just said–as one must so often in psychological discussion–about animals. As I wrote this I was reminded of a dream I once had in which I saw several little animals of great warmth and beauty, nuzzling each other and in good spirits. These animals were suddenly confronted with some unknown threat, whereupon they suddenly displayed wings, and flew flutteringly up into the sky. I was overawed with this event and realized that these little dog-like animals were angels!

When I reflected on the dream, I understood that angels, spirit creatures, also exist at the instinctual level, as Jung said. At bottom, spirit and instinct are one. There are only moments, however, when we fully realize that the struggle between instinct and spirit, our animal nature and spiritual nature, is really the battle of the opposites with one common base. In fairness, then, our fellow animals are surely not just the mechanical creatures that Descartes thought. There has been an evolution, however, which makes *homo sapiens* different from them in some ways.

Ever since the development of the neo-cortex among our ancestors or, alternately, the decision of Adam and Eve to disobey divine rules, there has been conflict between the instinctive motions of the soul (e.g. desire) and the cultural and psychological strictures against their enactment or fulfillment (spirit). Indeed, the interplay of spirit and instinct is experienced *in* the soul or psyche, and this is the stuff of our lives. Passion leads us to the word emotion, which means "to be moved out of," and emotion is what moves us out of our ordinary routine. It is also the psycho-physiological link between our bodily instincts and our mental constructions, realized in images.

Depth psychology, in particular, has focussed upon these passions of the mind. Indeed, the every attention to these passions is what lead to the discovery of the unconscious by Freud, and his recognition of the mechanism of repression, that trick we play upon ourselves to avoid experiencing those very painful passions which have harmed us in the past. As he went deeper, Freud found that a myth was at the core of the passions of love and lust, the Oedipus complex. Fixed as he was upon that one myth, the ground of his own psychology, he was unable to see that the entire basis of the psyche–and its ordering of the passions–rested in myths. It was Jung who discovered that the patterns of the psyche and, therefore, of behavior, gathered themselves in the stories of myth and that these were beautifully represented in the religions of humankind. Hence, it is not so surprising, after all, that our word for passion should be capitalized and used as the name for the chief myth of western culture, the passion of its outstanding divine representative.

Jung also demonstrated to us that the cultural stories, in myth and fairy tale and religion, reveal the workings of the soul. We need a key, however, a way to approach these stories so that we can better grasp their significance. With such a key, we can mitigate our passions, soften our suffering. This is usually accomplished through ritual: behavior is the healing way to gain access to the stories, without the need to understand them. (Hats off, here, to Behaviorists!) When ritual no longer suffices, when the meanings are no longer contained in the action, we then need a way into the background of it. The way is the symbol, as depth psychology has shown us, and the mode is interpretation. We retranslate the stories, so to speak, into the language of metaphor and symbol.

The "thirst" of the alcoholic, for example, was seen by Jung–when he helped give the idea to the founders of Alcoholics Anonymous–as a longing for the "spirit." The concentration of the symbol of "spirit" in "spirits," leading to addiction, was due to a lack of higher principle to connect with (the sense of deity). Fulfilling group life and ritual were also missing. So, it is not by chance that this insight helped to bring about one of the most effective antidotes to the modern scourge of alcoholism, Alcoholics Anonymous and its "twelve steps." Jung knew that an equivalent power of "spirit" was necessary.

It is probably not by chance that our day, which has witnessed a falling away from the effective impact of the "stories" of the religions, has also seen a concomitant rise in the addictions. The disintegration of our myths brings about both a return to fundamentalism (the longing for order and certainty) as well as the chaos of possession by passion (e.g. addictions).

One answer to this condition, particularly for a Jungianly-oriented psychotherapist, is to investigate the individual soul, to help each person in the discovery of and connection with his or her own myth. This search can also become a passion. The deeper we go with each person, the more we find that his/her myth is, in truth, also connected with the myths of humankind. The stories of the soul have a profound commonality, it turns out, not so unexpectedly, since we are, at bottom, much alike. Paradoxically, such efforts also reveal equally profound individuality. Commonality is balanced by difference, as examination of the world's religions might also have revealed to us.

So, individual leads to collective, which leads to the individual, and back again. This process is probably what the divine had in mind for us in the first place, according to the great Sufi mystic of Islam, Ibn Arabi. He saw that each of us carries a secret Name of the Divine, waiting to realize itself in our own unique, individual existence. None of us, not even the various religions, get the whole picture, but the sum of the Names constitute the Name of God. There is God in general (Allah) and our particular Name of Lord (Rabb); our task is to serve both. This is mightily like what people in long-term work with their own souls often find, too. They profit from looking at the parallels to their own dreams and fantasies in the religions and belief systems.

Because of this commonality, it is possible to read and write books which address the concerns of us all. So we come to the particular way that this book addresses the passions of the soul. I shall describe how it came about and then provide an outline, a guide whereby the reader can make this material of greater value to herself/himself.

Jung discovered a way to deal with the passions, which he called "Active Imagination." He describes this method in his essay on "The Transcendent Function" in Volume 7 of the Collected Works. Barbara Hannah has written a good book about this technique, *Encounters with the Soul*, and I have two essays on it in my little book, *The Nymphomaniac*. Jung's method was to have a dialogue with the unconscious, to engage his ego with whatever came in dream or fantasy which was a moving or troubling nature, such as passions. For example, if I am troubled by a rage reaction arising in response to someone blocking me on the freeway, I can turn and look at my rage, rather than engage in a dangerous competitive battle with the other chap or give him the hand-sign so dearly beloved these days. I allow the emotion to fill my being, but rather than express it outwardly, I enquire as to how it looks, what it intends, etc. As I do this, I see a fire swirling. This fire is both hot and cold. I wonder at this fact, and recognize that my rage is, indeed, both hot and consuming, but also cold an ruthless. In my fantasy, I put my hand in this flame, and discover that I am not burned. It feels like–dare I say it?–a divine fire. Excited, I realize that my rage at my auto-opponent arose as a result of the sense of my Self being trampled on, not my silly ego. And this Self need not engage in such a trivial pursuit as vengeance on that hapless creature. Now I remember a poem of Walter Savage Landor:

> *I strove with none, for none was worth my strife*
> *I warmed both hands before the fire of life*
> *It sinks, and I am ready to depart.*

The realization that I am only too ready to "strive" and that this is futile, now calms my rage and I am reconnected with this fire in my own soul, ready to employ it in better ways, such as right here.

Jung's method has proven to be very valuable for those who are looking for an ongoing relationship to their own passions and psyche generally. And so did I, for many years. After about sixteen years of this kind of work with myself, I found that the figures of my own active imagination now wanted to tell stories about their own quests and experiences, desiring my cooperation in this venture. As a result, I wrote two books of a kind of psycho-fiction. *The Tree: Tales in Psycho-mythology* had ten stories of individuation, pursued by people of different religious background and character; all of them had some passion to deal with. *The Quest*, the sequel to the *The Tree*, also had stories related to myths, but these were accomplished in pairs. When these two books were completed, another figure appeared, calling himself "The Grandson of the Knight," a third-generation hero of this spiritual path. The book which emerged, however, was no longer fiction. Rather, it was an encounter with various images and myths having to do with the passions, particularly those of lust and love. That provided the basis of the present book.

The narrator of Part I, then, is the Grandson of the Knight, who discovers, in his own active imagination, a Magician. This remarkable being is able to connect with and relive figures of history and myth, as well as literature. The Knight's painful struggle with his passions is thereby aided at a deeper level. His particular conflict between the two passions of lust and love unfolds into larger issues such as monogamy and polygamy, monotheism and polytheism, the One and the Many. At ever level, his passion is engaged.

With the help of the Magician, the Knight first interacts with the notorious figure of Don Juan, who embodies the "manliness" of love and lust. An interlude during this engagement with this dark side of lust and power comes in an examination of the tale of Bluebeard. Reliving these dark events of history and myth brings him, unexpectedly, to the Muses, who help him truly apprehend these abysses of the soul.

Following his immersion in the dark side of the passions, he undertakes an opposite path, that of Jesus and the Stations of the Cross. This Passion carries him deeper into Love's meaning, but it does not end there. The Magician carries him onward to the story of the Goddess of Love, Aphrodite, and the Knight, through her "stations," can apprehend feminine aspects of love, left-out in the masculine grasp of this passion. Finally, the figure of Eros is engaged and the Knight comes to a resolution of his issue of One and Many, love and lust, light and dark.

Part II of the book is now taken up with the work of the Daughter of Guinevere, a kind of alchemical sister to the Knight. She deals with the problem of "pairs," of opposites in relationships, in her struggle for individuation. To this end, she suffers the conflict of "sisters" (Belly and Heart), and takes up many of the pairs-stories in Greek mythology and religion, such as Father and Son, Father and Daughter (Zeus and Athema), Hecate, Husband and Wife (Zeus and Hera). She also immerses herself in the story of Mother and Son in a Christian context. She explores the mysteries of the Virgin Mary and her Rosary in detail. Finally, Mother and Daughter become resolved.

Volume Two continues the presentation, which now becomes increasingly clear as an attempt to build up an East-West Tree of Life, a kind of western psychological Kabbalah, in which the Greek myths, like those of the Hindu pantheon, find their place. Indeed, one of the most surprising discoveries of the work is the degree to which the Greek stories and gods, including their "stations," fit so well into an organization of western *chakras* (centers) and psychological functions. The psyche of the West has its own hidden order, much like that more explicitly described in the East.

Part III takes up the theme of the Group (after the One of the Knight and the Pair of Daughter of Guinevere). Now the two heroes combine forces, as alchemical brother and sister, in a mutual quest for wholeness. Maya the Yogini, from the East, comes to assist them as they undertake to connect with and interpret the tales of Dionysos, of Apollo, and of Hera.

Part IV, with the heading of "Union," carries the work onward by engaging the myths of Gaia and Kronos, Rhea and Zeus, Kronos and Zeus. The knowledge gained by such encounters requires a profound confrontation among the archetypes of Witch and Devil, Judge and Soul. Following this, they undergo a voyage among all the centers-chakras in both an eastern and western way, healing themselves thereby.

Part V, the culmination of the work, presents a schema of all the centers, along with the relevant Gods, psychological functions, types of consciousness and love, along with the animals and elements appropriate to each. "Hymns" to the various Gods are included. If this presentation is seen as comparable to certain Kabbalistic Tree of Life, or magical ones such as given by Dion Fortune in her book on the Magical Qabbalah, the author is pleased, for his intent is to continue that tradition, but with the significant admixture of the psychological information gained during the last century of depth-psychological work.

What began as a work with the passions became a passionate work. What started as a story emerged as a theoretical/practical schema, one meant to be inclusive. The task undertaken some twenty years ago in the stories of the Knight and his friends, found their conclusion in the non-fictional efforts of the Grandson of the Knight and his friends. The product of four years of labor was received with lack of understanding then, but recent years have seen changes in consciousness.

The reader's attitude might best be that of the second meaning of passion, namely, "receiving." He/she need only accompany these two heroes and respond as they do to the Gods and figures from literature and myth who come to life here as a result of the work of the Magician. If one has read *The Tree* and *The Quest*, so much the better, but it is not necessary. Bring only one's struggle with the passions and listen to how the alchemical brother and sister engage them.

If the readers find that their own myths are stimulated by these accounts and interpretations, so much the better. They might then make use of the hints given herein and embark upon their own voyage, perhaps using the final schema as a possible compass. It is enough, however, to absorb and react–in a "passionate" way!

A word must be added about the possible startle-effect of having a volume treating the sacred images of religions such as Christianity, Judaism, Buddhism and Hinduism on an apparent par with the ancient Greek religion and literary sources. I wish to affirm most forcefully that I mean no disrespect to any of these traditions; on the contrary, I am myself deeply immersed in them and am a "believer." Since my work as a Jungian analyst involves a religious attitude toward the psyche and its products, I can in no way discount or be disrespectful of the ground of the soul of us all, since it is made manifest in these self-same great religions. If a kind of "relativization" emerges, it does not mean that "anything is as good as everything" or that these stories are of equal value. The comparative approach puts the psyche as its center and respects it above all. If the reader, like me, is of the opinion that the psyche is created by the divine principle and finds its representation in its images, then he or she will know that respect for all does not involve reduction of value for any. Each person, each religion must find his/her/its own truth. The true purpose of psychological work in this area, it seems to me, is to enable us to emerge from this with a deepened appreciation of differences and similarities. Indeed, the very task undertaken by the pair of Knight and Guinevere is an ecumenical one, culminating in a "world myth," so to speak, without loss of difference and individuality. If religious feelings are hurt, I beg pardon at once, and hope that any such person so offended will permit me to present my own symbol without asserting that anyone need follow it. God speaks to us all in his/her own way. That, indeed, is the very theme of the book! I think it is not too utopian, however, to intuit that our globe is painfully inching toward such a world-story, honoring and treasuring, one hopes, all the varieties of our individuality and religious traditions.

J. Marvin Spiegelman
Studio City, California
Spring 1989

Preface and Introduction to
REICH, JUNG, REGARDIE & ME
THE UNHEALED HEALER
New Falcon Publications, First Edition, 1992

PREFACE

The Unhealed Healer is primarily a record of my experiences while undergoing the first four years of an eight year Reichian therapy with the famed chiropractor, occultist and Reichian therapist Dr. Francis Israel Regardie.

It details the "nuts and bolts" of procedure and content of very many of the sessions, along with reflections and fantasy work which I did on my own during those painful years of my mid-forties, almost twenty years ago.

Secondarily to this, and as means of an introduction, I have included a brief essay which I have entitled *BODY AND SOUL: REICH AND JUNG*. This paper is an inquiry into the body-soul problem by means of an examination of the work of Wilhelm Reich from the point of view of a Jungian analyst who has also had extensive Reichian work.

I explore Reich's personal and intellectual development, similarities and differences in the views of Reich and Jung, and their implications for the body-soul problem, with special reference to my own experience.

My credentials as a Jungian are as follows: eight years of Jungian analysis (upwards of seven hundred hours), training and graduation at the C.G. Jung Institute in Zürich (1959), and twenty-plus years of experience in private practice. My Reichian work consisted of eight years of personal therapy (about three hundred fifty hours), six years of practice, some seminars, but by no means as full a training as would be expected of an orgonomist.

The Unhealed Healer is aimed at psychotherapists, my fellow Jungians, Neo-Reichians, and to the patients of all of us, who might derive some solace, insight, fellow-feeling, and wonder, respectively. I do this with trepidation, of course, but my publisher and others think that this would be a extraordinarily useful thing to do.

Why, in heaven's name, am I foolhardy enough to do this? What dark motive of exhibitionism, masochism, or other ism lurks there to risk the judgment, opprobrium, scorn and contempt of my fellow healers or, just as bad, their pity? I must be out of my mind! Precisely. I undertook Reichian therapy to get "out of my mind" and into my body. I did not originally plan this. Rather, I had visited my future therapist, Francis Israel Regardie, along with my friend and colleague, L, to learn more about the general occult field, in which he was internationally known. When we spoke to him about our desire to learn more about that field, ("magic," sometimes spelled as "magick" to distinguish this spiritual path from entertainment), he responded that such powerful energies are released in magical work that it would be wise to undergo Reichian therapy first or along with our study, since "body-armor" causes great trouble when not released or resolved. We found his views convincing and undertook the work.

But why write about it, my fantasized interlocutor questions? I wrote for my own edification and because, for many years, before and since, I did so as part of my own developmental process. I even fancied myself as a potentially publishable writer of fiction, an "illusion" also documented in a companion volume of this series of "Failures," namely, *The Unpublished Writer*.

And why publish? Because I am in a unique position to withstand the anticipated scorn of colleagues and others. This is because I have "earned my dues" as a recognized clinical psychologist (Ph.D., University of California, Los Angeles, 1959, Diplomate, American Board, 1959) Jungian Analyst (Diplomate, C.G. Jung Institute Zürich, 1959), teacher (UCLA seven years plus seven at USC; lecturing in England, Japan, Israel, and the U.S.), consultant at hospitals, and successful private practitioner. I have also had published some sixty journal articles, and eleven books. So I seemed to have "arrived" and been successful, including areas of my personal family life. And this "success" was true! Also true was the fact of grief in my life, as everyone has, including the loss of my connection with professional colleagues at the time I undertook the Reichian therapy (repaired some years later). So I was unsuccessful as well.

A lot of the misery and pain shown in the record of this work, I think, was a result of the therapy itself. I am saddened as I look at the suffering chap I was, those years ago, but I am gladdened to be able to have compassion for him/me and to point out that the link-up with the body, as Jung taught us, and resides in the alchemical metaphor of our work, comes not so easily. My own pains with "body" and "world" were a paradigm for this psychological fact.

Secondly, I publish because most other patients can not or do not–and I was one in those years. Sure enough, I had had extensive personal and training analysis in Los Angeles and Zürich, to the tune of eight years, so I, like all analysts, knew what it meant to be a patient, but here I was, in an alien field, one I had previously held in contempt myself! My therapist was also trained as a chiropractor; another blow to my vaunted superiority! All of this was very useful to my re-definition and "embodying." My extensive previous Jungian analyses and practice had enabled me to embrace my soul and discover my Self, and there was no question of my deep and abiding commitment to what I had experienced in that work. Yet I clearly had troubles in connection with body and world, which Reichian therapy helped significantly, particularly the former; the latter is still in process, part of it is the risky appearance of this very book!

Thirdly, I publish because I am very skeptical of all accounts of what happens in therapy as reported by therapists. We all make use of events and conditions in our articles–I have done so myself–as if these were true or authoritative. Maybe so. But what does the patient think of all of this? How often (ever?) is there an article in which both patient and healer write about how and what they experienced in the work? Freud reported certain things about the Wolf Man which subsequently turned out to be utterly wrong and not nearly as favorable as he thought. Nor is he alone in this! I cringe when I think of those favorable incidents I have reported in articles, indicating significant change or cure which, subsequently, turned out not to be as I had imagined. I am sure that others have experienced something similar. Therefore, I write about my own experience, from the vantage point of one who is patient and therapist simultaneously. Surely there is value in this for some researcher, not so embodied in it all as I am, to advance our knowledge in this damnably complex and inter-subjective field where it is so difficult to arrive at mutually agreed-up verities.

So, I have convinced myself of the value of letting this book be published. It remains for the reader to make his own judgment. I can only add that the Unhealed Healer of this book wrote (and continues to write) a book about "Successes" and other developments in our healing profession and that these books will also ultimately appear. Finally I conclude this apologia with the heartfelt sharing of the pain and joy of this psychotherapeutic process, whether of body or of soul, whether one is patient or healer for, in truth, we are always both.

I want to salute my analysts and teachers, living and dead, healers all, and thank them. First and foremost C.G. Jung, followed by Max Zeller, Bruno Klopfer, Margaret McClean, C.A. Meier, Marie-Louise Von Franz, Liliane Frey, Rivkah Kluger, Hilde Kirsch, all Jungians. And latterly, come Wilhelm Reich and Francis Israel Regardie.

Finally, it is patients I thank. You have taught me everything!

J. Marvin Spiegelman
Fall 1991

INTRODUCTION

BODY AND SOUL: REICH AND JUNG

[The following paper was written in 1980, some time after my Reichian therapy was completed, and has not been published heretofore. It was an attempt to reconcile the views of the two researchers, aimed primarily at an audience knowledgeable about analytical psychology, to both inform them about Reich and compare him with Jung. It has been re-edited, in the spring of 1991, largely removing the quotations and diagrams drawn from Reich's original work. The reason for this is that those who are the inheritors of the copyrights of Reich's books and papers, I am informed, are extremely sensitive as to how this work is presented and who does so. They, I am told, are friendly neither to non-medically trained orgonomists, nor to those "spiritually" inclined. I belong to both categories. I can understand their sensitivity, since Reich was so maligned and misrepresented in life and after death, but I do regret not being able to present his own words. In the course of the presentation, I refer the reader to the relevant quotations.]

This paper is an inquiry into the body-soul problem by means of an examination of the work of Wilhelm Reich from the point of view of a Jungian analyst who has also had extensive Reichian work. My credentials as a Jungian are eight years of Jungian analysis (upwards of seven hundred hours), training and graduation at the C.G. Jung Institute in Zürich (1959), and twenty-plus years of experience in private practice. My Reichian work consisted of eight years of personal therapy (about thee hundred fifty hours), six years of practice, some seminars, but not the training undergone by orgonomists.

I will explore Reich's personal and intellectual development, similarities and differences in the view of Reich and Jung, and their implications for the body-soul problem, with special reference to my own experience.

REICH'S PERSONAL DEVELOPMENT

Wilhelm Reich was born on a farm in the German-Ukrainian part of Austria on March 24, 1897 to non-practicing Jewish parents. His childhood was atypical, for Jews of his time and place, in a number of ways; he rode horses, hunted, kept animals, had a private teacher who also helped him tend a laboratory for insects and plants. Even more atypical–and tragically so–was his experience of his mother's suicide when he was only fourteen. This self-destructive act happened after Reich told his father about his mother's affair with the boy's tutor. Three years later, Reich's father died of tuberculosis and the seventeen year-old was left alone to run the family farm. The enterprising and gifted young man managed this while also continuing his studies. World War I interfered with this work and he spent three years in the army where he rose to lieutenant and was decorated in Italy.

After the war, Reich attended medical school in Vienna, earning his living by tutoring fellow students. He also studied with Freud. Reich not only graduated with honors (1922), in four years instead of the six, he also was admitted to the Vienna Psychoanalytic Society in October 1920 while still a student!

Reich began a private practice in psychoanalysis and psychiatry in 1922, continuing his postgraduate education in neuropsychiatry for two years, under Professors Wagner-Jauregg and Paul Schilder. He was the first Clinical Assistant at Freud's Psychoanalytic Polyclinic in Vienna from its foundation in 1922, rising to its director in 1930. During this period, Reich became attracted to the social and sexual causation of neurosis and founded mental hygiene centers both in Vienna and Berlin, where he worked from 1930 to 1933.

It was during these years that he formulated his views on character analysis. He threw himself with vigor and energy into his work and into fighting political and social conditions he felt caused emotional crippling. He lectured on sexual hygiene and was outspoken on issues which are still hot and controversial today, such as abolition of laws against abortion, homosexuality and birth control. Seeing the misery, poverty and political inequities that he had not perceived previously, he became an advocate of social and sexual reform, even affiliating himself with Marxists and teaching at Workers' Colleges. He wanted to provide sex education, nurseries, and sex counselling facilities in factories and business, and advocated home leave for prisoners.

The reward for Reich's passionate work on these social and psychological issues in the nineteen twenties and early thirties was expulsion from both the International Psychoanalytic Association (1934) and the Communist Party. To what extent his own personality played a role in this rejection and to what extent his views caused it is not clear. But Reich himself noted that from early on among the psychoanalysts he thought himself as a sharp, killer fish among placid, less combative ones (10, p. 40). He was clever, opinionated, judgmental and arrogant, but Freud liked his vitality and intelligence. It seems that power-struggles as well as differences in viewpoint were the chief feature in his separation from these movements which had given him sustenance and a home.

In 1933, Reich left Germany to find a temporary haven in Oslo, Norway, where he continued his researches full time (giving up the private practice of therapy) until he was invited to the United States in 1939.

By 1942, Reich has acquired a two-hundred acre estate in Maine for his laboratory and research. He gave it the name "Organon," after the energy he believed he had discovered. Students came and some success, as well, but he was prosecuted by Federal Food and Drug Administration for his claims regarding his orgone energy accumulator. His defense that he was pursuing natural science and not conventional law was utterly unacceptable to the agency and his home was invaded, his books burned, his lab locked, and he was finally imprisoned, only to die there in 1957, a broken man. (The details of Reich's trial and jailing can be found in Jerome Greenfield's book, *Wilhelm Reich vs. the U.S.A.*, [1]. There is also a very beautiful personal book by Reich's son who lived through this period with him, called, *A Book of Dreams* [6].)

To read Reich's responses to the charges of the F.D.A. (9, Appendix), is to see a man fruitlessly engaged in a defense against the very forces he tried to combat throughout his life via education and reform. The gradual increase in suspicion, sense of persecution, feelings of extraordinary specialness and grandeur finally became quite pathological. Reich made extravagant statements about his powers, felt that UFO's were interested in his work, that President Eisenhower was secretly supporting him, and that he could significantly modify the weather. The extent to which his personality brought on his persecution, or that the real persecution that he received finally caused his deterioration, is hard to assess. I share the impression of Kovalenko and Brown 94) that no one was really willing or able to confront Reich at the "deep level of challenge and outspoken emotional exchange which was apparently natural and comfortable for him." This is particularly apparent in his interview about Freud (10), which we will discuss later on. Here, however, we must note that Reich's isolation and broken love bonds, experienced from early life onwards, and the tragic effects of moralistic judgment, haunted him throughout his life. He was attacked unmercifully and unfairly by individuals and groups who often twisted the spirit of his work. He was to comment on this activity in the concept of "emotional plague," which we will describe later.

REICH'S INTELLECTUAL DEVELOPMENT

Early in his career, Reich found that patients would talk endlessly about their symptoms and problems, but that when the possibility arose of changing the ways they lived or the structure of their personality, there was enormous resistance. He then shifted his attention to the analysis of the patient's character traits, much as symptoms had been worked with. By "character." Reich understood a stereotyped or characteristic way a person had of approaching life. This rigid responsiveness was seen as defensive in function and in the service of controlling and blocking off unacceptable feelings from within and, simultaneously, to defend against threats from outside. He called such modes of being "character armor" and found that these began early in life, later to become the foundation for neurosis and the blockage of any spontaneous response to life. The book, *Character Analysis* (7), appeared in 1929 and was both attacked and hailed, but was ultimately incorporated into the body of psychoanalysis. It was during this period (1923-1934) that he also developed his orgasm theory (see below), the idea of "statis neurosis," sex-economic self-regulation of primary natural drives as distinguished from secondary perverted drives, and explored the role of irrationalism and human sex-economy in the origin of political and personal dictatorship.

Most importantly, however, Reich extended his concept of psychic or character armor into that of muscular armor. By this idea, he meant that muscular tension and rigidities not only served the same purpose as did neurotic character structure, but that indeed they were functionally identical. A retracted pelvis is inhibitory of sexual drives as much s is a strait-laced attitude. The same holds true for a perennially sweet smile, or an elevated stiff chest; all serve to inhibit feelings and drives which training had labeled bad, e.g., rage, anxiety, resentments, sexual desire and, on the other hand, grief, love, pleasure, sympathy. Rigidity of musculature, in short, represents frozen emotion (5). This frozen emotion finds its expression in neuromuscular tension, postural defects and visceral disfunction.

Reich's therapy was devised gradually as he began to touch patients where he saw tension and rigidity. He gradually invented non-verbal techniques that penetrated bodily/armored resistance and had a reorganizing effect. The therapy is based on methods of breathing, movement, and relaxation which have the aim of dissolving the horizontal bands of tension which cross the body. He discovered these bands of tension which can be seen as segments: ocular, oral, neck, chest, diaphragm, abdomen, pelvis. Later researchers, such as Alexander Lowen, have, added the knees and the feet ("grounding".) In the respiratory block, for example, the person may have a chronic condition of holding the breath, or shallow breathing, originating in childhood fears and aimed at keeping control. Through the breathing methods in Reichian therapy, there is a gradual relaxing of this "holding," and the underlying feelings of anxiety, etc., can be released.

As the bands of tension dissolve, the autonomic nervous system becomes able to react strongly and powerful sensations, "streamings" (see below) and feelings emerge. Many people find such active sensations frightening and uncomfortable. If the therapy continues, however, the patient will ultimately find total release of tension, and experience what Reich referred to as the "orgasm reflex," a relaxation of the organism accompanied by a shivering, much as a cat does when it relaxes. This full release, occurring on the couch as the patient lets go of control, brings an enormous sense of well-being, re-organizes the character structure, and enables the individual to enjoy deep, open tenderness with others. Vulnerability is accepted, as well as the capacity to experience exchanges in which the core of their being is in connection with others. A natural sexuality is central in this exchange, as well as natural morality.

A person's armor is what either precludes sensations which should be erotic or pleasurable, or prevents build-up and discharge alike, leaving people in a chronic condition of unreleasable tension. Aggression and hate are among the few emotions that heavily armored people express. Their eroticism is converted into hate, just as does the surrounding armored culture. One of the most characteristic changes in Reichian therapy is that people begin to refuse to continue relationships which were exploitative, battering, or injurious. Yet the culture is full of such negative relationships, and Reich called the collective condition of armor the "emotional plague." He felt that such a label was accurate because of its chain-like reaction, when people are involved with flurries of truth-twisting, rumors, gossip, persecution and automatic rejection of the new, as well as a fear of freedom.

The very vivid tingling sensations which people experience in therapy, called "streamings," along with clonisms and other somatic phenomena, occurring in various regions of the body, become expressions of the bio-electric energy which Reich felt he had discovered. This quite concrete development of the libido idea, Reich called "orgone." At first, Reich recognized that these tingling feelings and prickling sensations were caused by the free-flowing orgone which had been kept latent because of the chronic muscular tensions.

Gradually, by experimentation, Reich concluded that these energies also existed external to people. He believed that the had discovered an energy which is part of the living, pulsating world, a basis and source of life. This bio-electric energy streams among persons, earth's environment and the stars. There is, therefore, a cosmic stream of orgone energy which can be experienced in the organism, demonstrated in the laboratory, visible as "bions" and as seen in the atmosphere.

From 1940 onwards, Reich's work shifted from a clinical and therapeutic interest to what he felt was an increasingly biological and natural science endeavor. This resulted in increasing ostracism and antagonism toward him. Notable here was his work in cancer (*The Cancer Biopathy*, excerpted in the Writings, 9). He felt that cancer was a matter of biological frustration, an organismic shrinking and withdrawal, which occurred, as did other somatic diseases, in just those areas where armoring was most severe. This view of cancer, along with his use and advocacy of an "orgone energy accumulator"–a box-like device he believed could increase the orgone energy surrounding a person and help to relieve illness–brought on the wrath of the medical establishment.

As if these threats to current biological and medical thought were not enough, he also researched an area which he called "cosmic orgone engineering" (C.O.R.E.), which led him to speculations about smog, storm-control, weather in general, drought and desert conditions. He even produced a tentative technique for the production of rain in arid areas.

I am in no position to evaluate his biological and engineering research, but it is relevant to note that the attack which he received for his views was formidable–even though he described in detail how his experiments were conducted and asserted a natural science basis. None of his critics sought to replicate his work. This attack finally led to his imprisonment and death: a concrete and tragic example of emotional plague.

It is important to ask how isolated was Reich in what he discovered? His energy concept is remarkably similar to that described in East Indian, Asian, and western occult literature, even to the parallel of his armor segments with the chakra centers. Reich's vegetative streamings are not unlike the vertical meridians of acupuncture or the energy experienced in Kundalini Yoga. Reich seemed not to know of these parallels. Indeed, he showed no interest in comparing his findings and views with other material in contemporary or ancient physiology or psychology. His biological conception of core and periphery seems overly simple to biologically trained people, and his language often seemed too authoritarian and alienating.

Yet his work was vast and profound. All the body therapies of today owe much of their origin in his thinking and discoveries. Reich's personal and social isolation was tragic an done still does not know when his theories and discoveries can be put to an adequate outside test.

REICH AND JUNG: SIMILARITIES AND DIFFERENCES

I begin this discussion of Reich and Jung, regretfully, with Reich's feeling about Jung, to whom he, like many others, erroneously attributed both a naive, unscientific mysticism and anti-semitism. In the interview with him by Kurt Eissler (10, pp. 88-89), Reich said that Jung was correct in discovering a universal libido or energy, but Freud was right in saying that it was unscientific. Reich believed that he, himself, had proved it scientifically, being able to measure it with a Geiger counter, thus taking away its "mystical" connotation. Reich also merely accepted that Jung was labelled anti-semitic, without further inquiry.

Reich continues the misconception in *The Function of the Orgasm* (8, p. 127), in which he criticizes Jung for taking all the sexual aspect out of the concept of the libido and ending up with the concept of the collective unconscious, which Reich saw as merely mystical or in line with Nazi ideology.

Great men do not always read each other and, alas, may not understand their rivals any better than the rest of us do. But, in fairness, Reich did not have access to such works as that of Jaffe (3), who corrects in depth that mistaken impression of anti-semitism or national socialist predilections. He could have seen an earlier corrective effort by Ernest Harms, however, in 1946 (2).

Despite this negative judgment, there are a number of ideas or areas in which Reich comes close to formulating his conclusions quite parallel with those of Jung. The first of these is to be found in the basic formulation of opposites (see 9, p. 102). He observed that neurotic patients develop stiff body peripheries, while maintaining an inner core of aliveness. Such patients feel uncomfortable within themselves, inhibited, unable to be themselves, feel cut off. Sometimes they are so tense with this unexpressed energy that they feel like bursting; they long to move toward the world, but can not do so. These efforts toward contact with life are frequently so painful that disappointments are unbearable and the person prefers to crawl into himself. Reich concludes from this that the basic biological function of moving outward toward the world and life is counteracted by a moving away from it, or a withdrawal into self.

A moment later, Reich notes that these opposites are to be particularly noted in a functional antithesis between sexuality vs anxiety to the simplest terms: the fundamental pair of opposites are the sympathetic and parasympathetic nervous system.

Reich continues the discussion of polarities in his *Function of the Orgasm* with the chapter heading, "Pleasure (expansion) and anxiety (contraction): Primary antithesis of Vegetative Life." In this chapter, he reports that by 1933 he recognized a unity between psychic and somatic functioning. He makes it a cardinal point that the primary biological opposites of contradiction and expansion are identical in both the somatic and psychic realms. He goes on to present tables of comparisons, such as the antithesis between potassium (parasympathetic) and calcium (sympathetic) in the autonomic nervous system as variants of expansion and contraction. He notes that parasympathetic innervations are accompanied by dilatation, turgor, pleasure, etc. whereas sympathetic nerves come into play whenever there is contraction, blood is withdrawn from the periphery, pallor and pain appear. He concludes from this that life itself is a continuous process of expansion and contraction, pleasure and joy in moving out of self toward the world, and sadness and contraction in moving away from it, into the self (9, p. 125-6).

In later books, *Ether, God and Devil* and *Cosmic Superimposition* (in 9, p. 299 for quote), Reich subsumes these oppositions in a basic principle, pulsation. Pulsation, he says, is the fundamental characteristic of orgone energy, itself, which can be then be subdivided into two opposite and antagonistic part-functions–expansion and contraction. One can also synthesize orgone energy from them, he says, most interestingly.

We can readily see that Reich, like Jung, was very much impressed by the polarities in nature and the psyche, but, with his biological bent (even bias?), he saw these as expressions of the autonomic nervous system and the pulsation of life itself. I think this is a useful extension of Jung's polarities and may suggest some research of a physiological nature into Jung's introversion-extraversion typology. Reich's partial bias, I think, can be seen in his equation of displeasure with the introverting aspect of the polarity, although I do not think that he was an extravert. If so, how did he manage to get himself into such terrible difficulty with the world around him? His biological reductionism, however, also shows itself in his rejection of meaning, purpose or goal. In several places (e.g. 9, p. 104) he says that biology knows only functioning and development, follows a natural course without any other significance. Such a view fits better with a traditional biology than with psychology, where the archetype of meaning is already supplied with the archetype of the spirit. It seems to me that, later in life, Reich came closer to the meaningful perspective with his conception of bio-psychological unity, as we shall see.

We may now look at Reich's extension of his bio-psychological polarities into what one might call his "basic symbol crops up in several different books and with different pairs of opposites. In it, he formulates a process of initial unity, followed by differentiation and opposition, followed by a tendency toward another, higher level of unity. This Hegelian variation of thesis-antithesis-synthesis was also a basis of Jung's thought, as we know. The diagram that Reich used for depicting psychosomatic identity and antithesis can be visualized as a basic dot, considered the source of biological energy, out of which rises an arrow, representing this same identity, which then separates into a pair of opposites, psyche and soma, carrying the opposition (e.g. 9, p. 106). Later on, he uses a similar diagram in connection with the autonomic nervous system (9, p. 132). The lower arrow is now vegetative life itself and the opposites are the sympathetic and parasympathetic systems.

In a later book, *The Cancer of Biopathy* (9, p. 260), Reich again uses his schema to describe his orgone therapy as neither a psychological nor a physiological-chemical therapy. Instead he sees it as strictly biological therapy having to do with disturbances of pulsation in the autonomic system. In this diagram, the opposites are mechanical lesion and chemical-physical therapy on the somatic side, with psychotherapy and neurosis on the side of the psyche.

Reich uses this diagram not only in the opposition psyche-soma, the nervous system and in healing. he continues to employ it in a distinction between "good" and "evil"–in the sense of good and bad energy (9, p. 456). "Dor" is the evil energy. Reich is here referring to the antagonism inherent in life energy functions themselves. Evil, he feels arises out of stalemated or immobilized life energy.

Reich's trinitarian symbol–if one can use such a term for his intensely biological imagery–leads over into a four-fold formulation as he discusses the phases of his "orgasm formula": mechanical tension–electrical charge–electrical discharge–mechanical relaxation (p. 114). It is this four-fold system that leads him into using images of union, of circles and spheres.

There are remarkable statements, even in his early and classic *Character Analysis* (9, pp. 148-150) which only too clearly present a representation of the image of the uroborous, of the organism as snake biting its own tail! He describes the organism, particularly in the experience of the orgasm, as striving to unite together head and tail, the embryologically important mouth and anus. This is so fundamental as to be basis of the orgasm reflex. He presents a drawing which resembles a worm with head and tail trying to come close together and calls this the emotional expression of the orgasm reflex. When the organism surrenders itself to its sensations of flowing, it can also surrender itself completely to the partner in the sexual embrace.

Reich then asks what function is served by this moving together of the two ends of the trunk, making for this orgasmic pulsation? He then asserts that the answer goes deeper than the individual biological organism. He sees this as suprapersonal, but not metaphysical nor spiritual. All the same, Reich's denial does not stop him from calling that yearning for surrender and union, "cosmic." He goes on to say that if these two ends of the trunk bend backward, away from each other, instead forward and toward one another, the organism will not be capable of surrendering itself to any experience, whether love or work. Muscular armor, the result of this lack of surrender, essentially prevents this orgasm reflex.

That the symbol of the snake biting its own tail, the uroborous, so dear to alchemy and to Jung, should also be at the base of Reich's work, is remarkable. But since he, too, is struggling to get a grasp of the psyche in matter and its biology, it may not be so surprising after all.

It may also not be surprising when we find that the circle becomes a central image for Reich, both in his depiction of the egg-shape of the "orgonome," the basic form of living matter, and in his portrayal of pathology. For example, he describes (9, p. 337) the most conspicuous aspect of the orgasm reflex—the coming together of mouth and genitals—as having led him to the origin of the orgonome form, which is a circle. He had noted the orgasmic convulsions of animals or the swimming of jellyfish in such a way that the body tends to sag in the centre, facilitating this union.

Reich frequently uses the circle symbol, from center to periphery, with the impulse coming from the center, to be deflected by a circle of armor into deviations (e.g. 9, p. 132). When Reich describes his idea of "superimposition" in the genital embrace, one clearly apprehends a biological level of the *coniunctio* archetype (9, pp. 354-355). He describes the preorgasmic body movements, particularly the orgasmic convulsions, as extreme attempts of the organisms and their energy to fuse with each other. He even avers that the orgone energy, in such cases, actually succeeds in transcending the limits of material orgonome. This reaches, I think, a clear perception of the desire of the ego to transcend itself in what Reich previously rejected as mystical experiences. He finally can speak of orgasmic longing as a yearning to strive beyond one's self, and even becomes the answer to riddle of why dying is often represented in the orgasm (9, p. 355). In increasingly poetic language, Reich brings forward the mystical ideas of "salvation in the hereafter," "liberating death" and even nirvana, as ways of expressing that the naturally functioning organism is fulfilled in the orgasm reflex and in the sexual superimposition that accompanies it.

Reich's disclaimer not to the contrary, the *coniunctio* image is deeply imbedded in this concept. This will be even more clearly seen below as I discuss his later understanding of Christ. At this point, it may suffice to indicate that there are several crucial images which Jung has written about extensively and which form the core to Reich's attempt at making psychology biological.

I turn now, to other views of Reich which are of interest to a Jungian. His view of fantasy, for example, which he earlier decried in the sexual act (9, p. 210), is contained in the statement that a person can not imagine anything that does not have a real or objective existence in one form or another, since sense perception is a part of the natural functionings of organisms and follows natural laws, hence "real."

And how is fantasy real? Self perception is an essential part of the life process, says Reich. Very much along the lines of Jung, one might say, and yet a very far cry, indeed, from the elaborate and differentiated way that Jung worked with image and fantasy and their archetypal roots. Could one not venture the guess that what Jung had worked out on the psychological (soul) level, Reich was working on at the biological (body) level? I shall examine this question later on.

There are very real differences between the two thinkers, however, which can be seen, for example, in Reich's view that the function of sensation is everything. Jung said that there are at least three other ways of apprehending existence: feeling, thinking, and intuition. Reich's idea of functionalism transcended both mechanistic thinking and mysticism, however. He noted that science came to the realization that sensation was the key to outstanding nature, that that function is the bridge between the ego and the outer world (9, p. 281). The unity of psyche and soma, he referred to as the principle of orgonomic functionalism and this unity, of emotion and excitation, of sensation and stimulus, was its basis. He rejected any form of transcendentalism, he said (9, p. 291), although we have seen where his language goes beyond this.

Reich had no use for a mechanistic attitude toward the body-psyche, which for him was an indication of an armored condition, nor for mysticism, which he saw as merely a consequence of the blocking of direct organ sensations and the subsequent manifestation of these sensations as pathological perception of supernatural powers (9, p. 293).

This leads us into other examples of Reich's view of religion. He believed that, since enduring suffering is the result of the organic incapacity for pleasure, religious ecstasy was essentially masochistic–that is to say, release from sin was the same as release from inner sexual tension. Since the armored person can not do this himself, release is desired or expected from an all-powerful authority, namely God (9, pp. 97-8). Reich, no doubt correct about some suffering, stated that his formulation applied to all religions and suffering, therefore performing the kind of reductionism he learned from Freud.

A fuller statement of his views about religion and sexuality is to be found in his work on orgonomic functionalism (9, p. 305). There, he says that the sharp distinction between sexuality and religion leads to their irreconcilability, and is to be found in both mechanistic and mystical thinking. This is carried to such extremes that the Catholic Church, for example, sees sexual pleasure as a sin, even when sanctified by marriage. The functionalist resolves this contradiction of nature in one's own organism. When natural sexual expressions were repressed in the human animal during the development of the patriarchy, this produced a severe, unbridgeable contradiction between sexuality as sine and religion as liberation from sin. In primitive religions, says Reich, religion and sexuality were not separated, were one. With the patriarchy, this was split into sin and God. The functionalist understands the identity of emotions in sexuality and religion, the origin of the estrangement and the dichotomy it created, as well as the fear of sexuality among religious people. He also understands the degeneration of sexuality in pornography. The mechanist and the mystic are a product of this contradiction, remain trapped in it, and perpetuate it. The functionalist breaks through the barriers of this rigid contradiction by finding the common features in emotion, origin, and nature.

This is a clear statement by Reich which, like the previous reduction, leaves us seeing its limitations. His understanding of religious experience is small and he projects wholeness onto primitives. But Reich is clear in taking his stand on the image of a "natural" religion based on a "natural" biology. We shall see later on how well this vision was to sustain him. But now we can follow how his intended biological and functional thinking begins to take on other imagery. For example, in that same book (9, p. 317), he believed that he had found the answer to the hatred and destructive thinking of both mechanistic and mystical thinking: this was the realm of the devil.

This equation of the sadism and destruction, attendant upon armoring, with the Devil, finds its counterpart when Reich, in his later book on the Emotional Plague (9, p. 473), equates "life" with Christ. There, he wishes to subsume, under the heading "murder of Christ," the hatred of all that is alive. For Reich, Christ becomes the principal of life itself, free of armor and, therefore, like a red flag for a bull. A far leap for the functionalist, one thinks. And was it not also Reich's fate to be "crucified," because in his own way he tried to support and identify with this "principle of life" against those who he claimed supported armor and the emotional plague, the "devil?"

I want to turn now to some other areas which show a similarity between Reich's conclusions and Jung's. Here, first, are Reich's views on energy knowing itself (9, p. 517). He not only thinks that the very quest for knowledge is the attempt of orgone energy in the living organism to know itself, to become conscious, but it, itself, is a piece of that cosmic orgone energy in action. Becoming almost rhapsodic, once more, Reich feels that he has touched upon the greatest riddle of life, namely that of self-perception and awareness. All striving for perfection appears as a striving for integration of emotion and intellect, for the greatest freedom and flow of bioenergy without blockage. In this quest, one becomes aware that the self is only a bit of organized cosmic orgone energy and, from a more profound perspective, is a step in the functional development of the cosmic orgone itself.

This statement of cosmic orgone energy becoming aware of itself is very much like that of Jung's, is it not, of the Self knowing itself through the encounter with the human ego? Reich even goes so far as to recognize this process as a religious one (p. 518): He even says that the human animal will slowly get used to the fact that he has discovered his God and can now begin to learn the ways of God in a very practical manner. Still later, in describing his own developing experiences, but in an impersonal way, Reich says that the image of God, at one point, appeared to be the perfectly logical result of man's awareness of the existence of an objective functional logic in the universe (p. 521). Reich's discovery of this "functional logic" the approaches Jung's formulation of synchronicity (pp. 522-23), when he states that there is a functional identity of objective and subjective natural logic, which is active and of which the investigator felt himself to be a faithful tool. Reich even admits that he followed this path whereever it led him, with awe, as well as a deep sense of responsibility and humility. He uses the image of a "symphony" to express this identity of biological and cosmic superimposition. If these thoughts do not constitute a religious connection with the soma-psyche and universe, then there is none!

I would like to close this section, describing Reich's views as they become similar to some of Jung's, with a paraphrase of a statement which is an eloquent support of what Jung would call individuation (9, pp. 504 ff). There he advises us to follow our own truth, as if it were our brain or liver and in no way try to live a truth which is not fully our own. He also advises us not to preach, but to live our truth and, thereby, by example, show people how to find their own way to truthful living. No two truths are alike, there are no absolutes, but there are some which are common to all. All trees have roots in the soil. For example, but no tree can draw on the roots of another for nourishment. Therefore, we have to find our own. The way to do this is by listening patiently to ourselves. This does not lead to chaos, but to the place where all common truth is found, the sap common to all living things, beyond animal and man. In a final poetic burst which, for the present reviewer, constitutes evidence that Reich did, indeed, find his truth, he enjoins us to forgo other prophets and attend to how we feel when we love dearly, when we are creative or build our home, give birth to our children or look at the stars at night.

DISCUSSION

As we watch the change in Reich's views over time, we see an anti-religious, anti-mystical viewpoint change to expressions which are almost ecstatic in style, if not in content. Yet this ecstatic and hortatory style does not escape a deep pessimism about the possibility of therapy, including his own, to change anything, really, in the human condition. When interviewed by Eisler in 1952, Reich went so far as to say that there was no use in individual therapy at all, except to help a little bit here and there or for therapists to make money. But for the larger, social situation, it was hopeless. That was why he gave it up. Only in infants was there any hope, in unspoiled protoplasm (10, pps. 46-47).

One see's Reich's despair at the impossibility of changing the social conditions that make for armor and neurosis. We can hardly blame him when we consider that all the insights of depth psychology over the last century have had hardly any impact on the world's social condition at all! Yet is such hopelessness totally warranted? Jung did not seem to think so, which I will discuss in a moment. Let us first continue with these observations from Reich, but now bringing his experiences in connection with Freud, who also was rather despairing about the ultimate capacity of analysis to modify people fundamentally.

Reich tells Eisler that when he first heard Freud say that it was not the purpose of the therapist or anyone else to save the world, Reich disagreed. But, after many years of agony and suffering emotional plague from people's armor, Reich agreed. He came to this agreement only after attempting the changes; Freud gave up without trying.

In this book, Reich makes a considerable point of Freud's pessimism, based on his failure to resolve the character armor resident in his structure, but this did not prevent Reich from arriving at the same conclusion. He continues (10, pp. 69-70) on the topic of therapy, telling how treatment at the beginning of his career was three months, on the average, becoming longer and longer, until Freud left therapy altogether. Freud was clearly disappointed. Reich came to the same conclusion, he tells us, but only after much experience. In his view, adults are hopeless. He uses the analogy, once more, of a tree. Once it has grown crooked, you can't straighten it out. Then Reich startlingly concludes that the biological plasma of the human race has been spoiled for millennia!

Why then, do we pay attention to the views of Freud and Reich if they, at the end, became so pessimistic about the possible benefits of therapy? Because, I think, they discovered partial truths, if not whole truths. They have advanced psychological understanding and thinking in depth, an innovation which has had considerable reverberation far beyond the impact they experienced during the course of their lives. If they have not deeply effected the political world, they have at least effected the growing corps of therapists and their patients.

For those of us to whom the Jungian viewpoint—with its lack of scientific materialism and its freedom from dogmatism—is more congenial, we can appreciate what these thinkers have to offer. In the present context, I am particularly impressed with Reich's penetration into the body and its tensions, rigidities, and energies. For me, Jung expanded in the depths of the soul the initial discovery of Freud of the unconscious, and Reich has deepened that discovery into the body.

My own experiences of Reichian therapy leads me both to appreciate and agree with what Reich found. It was very clear to me, from the outset, that the breathing and movement techniques of Reichian therapy brought me into contact with my own body rigidities and the possibility of their relief. The resultant deep affects and experiences were not different in kind from those I experienced in Jungian analysis, but they were certainly dissimilar in the quality of connecting these affects most intimately with body sensations. One might say that, for me, as an introverted intuitive type, the Reichian method helped me to get even more in touch with my fourth function of sensation than did the usual Jungian methods of reflection, dream interpretation and active imagination. This procedure of working from the body directly, from sensation and movement to image, rather than the reverse, as usually happens in active imagination, was valuable for me.

Yet I am also in agreement about the limits of Reichian therapy. I did not experience, for example, a final orgasmic reflex about which Reich speaks, although this did occur periodically. After every session there was considerable relaxation, relief and deepening of connection with a psycho-biological core of being. Yet these periods of wholeness were relatively brief, and soon there was a return to some experience of tension, armor, rigidity in some region of my body. Was this because of my own nature, perhaps? Did the astrological condition in my horoscope (Grand Square of Fixed signs) contribute to this situation in a particular way? Or was it a measure of physiological inheritance? A physitrist (an orthopedic specialist) was of the opinion that people of eastern European origin had more muscular rigidity and stiffness than other groups. Or was it some other aspect of my individual psychology? I think that all of this is true, in large measure. Yet my observation of other patients who have undergone Reichian therapy and even those who may be said to have achieved permanent orgasmic reflex leads me to believe that they are no more free and unarmored than are the bulk of Jungians individuated!

I have written elsewhere (11, p. 101-116) that each therapeutic modality seems to have something specific to offer, yet each system's result seems to entail its opposite, failure! So that, for example, Freudians do not seem to be sexually freer or more genitally mature than others, nor are Adlerians less free of the power drive, nor Reichians less rigid, nor are Jungians more individual. Yet those of us who adhere to a viewpoint or a system have obviously gained considerably from our work therewith.

My conclusion is that each of us, and each view, have some piece of a larger totality of the human experience, just as the various religions seem to apprehend the divine in a particular way. Insofar as we can experience these various therapeutic approaches and findings in ourselves, we transcend provincialism. There are probably as few of us who can do this as there are people who can appreciate the divine experience in the variety of religions! Still, some of us need to try and, for the sake of the evolution of human consciousness, there may be some merit in explicating some of the overlap. It is in this connection that I see Reich and Jung.

Reich, from my standpoint, presents the possibility of expanding Jung's idea of psychic energy, libido, into the biological and body domain directly. It is not by chance, in my opinion, that so much of Reich's conceptions as to the polarities of psychobiology, of synchronicity, of the value of the individual, of freedom and the need to experiment with one's nature, are congenial with Jung's view. I suspect that both men experienced a certain depth of the soul by going deeply into themselves, and both suffered difficulty in communicating their findings and gaining recognition in their lifetimes. Yet we who follow need not be stuck in parochialisms.

I can aver, for example, that it was very clear to me, lying on that Reichian couch for many years, that the "screamings: and flow of energy that I experienced thereon was a most concrete and viable example of the psychic energy that I had for years encountered in terms of images in dreams, fantasies and affects. "Fourth function" or no, this coming to grips with the direct experience of body-energy in the form that Reich describes is most convincing, just as the direct impact of the archetypes can be experienced if one seriously commits himself or herself to the process of active imagination. How these two quite empirical approaches of the soul can then be linked up with the traditional experiences in kundalini yoga, kabbalistic meditation techniques, occult practices and the like remains to be accomplished. I can only say that it is to be regretted that Reich seemed not to know that the energy he described had also been experienced by others in many traditions. He, however, was unique in showing a technique whereby this can readily be produced, and he was also a pioneer in linking such energy and its blocking to the segments and their armoring.

I would like to see further research done in the area of the energies. For example, the linking of typology with autonomic nervous system dominance would be helpful. Yet the basic research for therapists, of course, is with ourselves and with our patients. It is in the spirit of sharing these findings with other therapists that I present this paper.

For me, there is no doubt that the Jungian perspective and findings are the most congenial to my own psychology and experience. Yet it was particularly in the area of my own fourth function, sensation, that the Jungian perspective seemed (and still does seem) insufficient. I was personally helped by Reichian therapy to improve my awareness of sensation, both introverted and extroverted, but I still see little impact from any of the depth psychologies on the facts of the world (extraverted sensation function), the environment, or the societies in which they live. This is not the fault of these psychologies, but it is incumbent upon us to recognize, as do Brown and Kovalenko (4, pp. 10-11) that

> There is growing existential despair, disillusion with authorities, continued arms build up, inflation, ecological and environmental disaster, terrorism, inability to solve starvation and world health problems or apply the wonders our technology has produced to practical world conditions. It should not be surprising that people are filled with anxiety, depression and stress.

Given such a condition of existence, both Freud and Reich grew pessimistic, even bitter. Jung, on the other hand, seems to have had a sufficiently large world-view to take in the obvious negativities and transcend them. He did this by linking up his own experiences historically and cross-culturally, so that he felt less isolated and alone. He also did so, I believe, by grappling with the problem of evil in a psychological and historical manner which helped him see our condition as an evolutionary one. His magnificent book, Answer to Job, is one that revolutionized our understanding of the problem of evil and made it available to us as a psychological problem with which an individual can grapple. With Jung, therefore, one can struggle with these issues in the depths of one's own soul. It is from our own work with evil that an enhanced consciousness can result in some change in the collective, inner or outer.

At the day to day level of therapeutic work, I can report that I have used Reichian methods, either alone or in conjunction with Jungian work, with perhaps one-quarter of my patients over a period of six years. More recently, I have generally given up Reichian methods and look to find other ways and views whereby sensation, body and world can impact my analysands and myself within the traditional analytical work. I do this partly from the realization that I am not as skilled or as "natural" as Reichian as I would like, and partly because the asymmetrical stance of the therapy (doctor "treating" or "working on" the patient) is less congenial to me at this time than the work in symmetry (mutual process). This in no way leads me to value the Reichian work less, any more than I denigrate the traditional asymmetric stance of Freudian and Jungian colleagues. Rather, I do this from a sense of individual talent and temperament. I am strongly of the opinion that a knowledge and experience of Reich's work would be of great value to many Jungians–as great, perhaps, at the physical level, as the knowledge of alchemy has been at an intellectual level.

REFERENCES

1. Greenfield, Jerome. *Wilhelm Reich vs. The U.S.A.* W.W. Norton & Co., New York, 1974
2. Harms, Ernest, "C.G. Jung –Defender of Freud and the Jews." *Psychiatric Quarterly*, April 1946.
3. Jaffe, A. "C.G. Jung and National Socialism" in *From the Life and Work of C.G. Jung.* Harper and Row, New York, 1971.
4. Kovalenko, Lawrene and Brown, D. "A Talk about Reich, Jung, and Contemporary Times" for Saddleback Community College, May 1979.
5. Regardie, Francis. *A Chiropractic Theory for the Emotional Disorders.* (privately printed, no date)
6. Reich, Peter. *A Book of Dreams.* Harper and Row, New York, 1973.
7. Reich, Wilhelm. *Character Analysis.* Orgone Institute Press. New York, 1949. (Original in 1933 and 1929)
8. Reich, Wilhelm. *The Function of the Orgasm.* Noonday Press, New York, 1971. (Original in 1927 and 1942)
9. Reich, Wilhelm. Selected Writing. Farrar, Strauss and Giroux, New York, 1973.
10. Reich, Wilhelm. *Reich Speaks of Freud.* Farrar, Strauss and Giroux, New York, 1967.
11. Spiegelman, J. Marvin. "The Image of the Jungian Analyst and the Problem of Authority." *Spring*, 1980, pp. 101-116.

An Introduction to
RIDER HAGGARD, HENRY MILLER & I THE UNPUBLISHED WRITER
New Falcon Publications, First Edition, 1997

As the title suggests, this is a sad book. It is a record of the experiences and reflections of an unpublished writer–myself–as he finally finds a publisher for his work, but one who turns out to be incompetent or fraudulent or both But this is also a funny book. It starts out being the adventure of the writer's encounter with a dead author, H. Rider Haggard, and an Angel, all of whom go to the Land of Tewfik wherein a Green Man and an Orange Lady hold sway. This has got to be funny, I think, at least in the sense of "peculiar," if not also "ha-ha." Furthermore, our unhappy, unpublished writer is welcomed there and honored very highly. Finally, this is something of a mysterious book, taking up issues of fantasy and reality, good and evil, spirit and matter, vanity and service, ego and Self.

As I look at the book now, some twenty years since I undertook the writing of it, I realize why I began this introduction as if I were writing about another person: it is both I and not-I. The "Unpublished Writer" that I was then has been superseded by one who has fifteen books to his credit and the sadness and defeat have given way, too, to a sense of joy and fulfillment. Perhaps present readers, especially other "unpublished writers," will take heart from this. That period, the early 1979s, was a time when I wrote *Reich, Jung, Regardie & Me: The Unhealed Healer*,

(New Falcon Publications, 1933) a "true story," like that of the Writer, but including a relation with the fantasy world also. How could I not, as a Jungian, be deeply involved with the imagination? I also wrote about "The Empty Teacher" and "The Unfrocked Priest" at that time, fantasy figures but related to life experiences as well. This group of failures finally came together with the "Powerless Magician." Out of that came a book entitled *Failures and Successes*, which will also appear in due course.

Some people, particularly writers, might like to know how this all came about. In my teens, I had the writerly desire, as do many, and fulfilled this by working on my junior and senior high school newspapers and yearbooks, as well as writing stories. During my years as a sailor in the Merchant Marine during World War II, ages eighteen to twenty, I wrote a book about my experiences. I hoped to get it published, finish college, and then go back to sea, writing stories and shorter works, being able to write a "deep" book at the age of forty. I thought I was a second Jack London. When my book failed to get published, I turned to another profession, ultimately becoming a psychologist and Jungian analyst. I felt as passionate about this as I had been about writing, and was surprised, when I turned forty, that I was moved to write fiction again, calling it "psycho-mythology."

For several years I was deeply absorbed in this writing, which made up for my loneliness when I felt the inner necessity to resign from my local professional group and wrote three books. I was pleased with the result and was gratified, too, when my friend, the writer Henry Miller, also found it worthwhile. Even Anais Nin, whom I knew only casually, supported my writing by asking her publisher to consider the work. Despite this encouragement, I received some forty rejections from as many publishers, a numbing and ego-reducing experience, as most writers know. At last, a small, local publisher was found, with whom I was to publish the first one, *The Tree*, as a joint venture. At the same time, I dreamed that H. Rider Haggard, a writer whose worked touched my imagination very much, came to me from the dead, looking for a relationship. The present book begins at this point.

What might it mean that an "unpublished writer" book needed to get written and published? I think that it, like the "Unhealed Healer" book, was necessary as an experience of failure, one that many who undergo it and few can express, thus also serving as a possible solace (and even a source of merriment) for those who endure such painful conditions. I hope so. In any case, it is to those suffering writers, published and unpublished, that I dedicate this book. In particular, I want to pay tribute to my friend, Helen Janiger, a writer who wrote voluminously but grew ill and died before she could see her work in print (except for one small jewel of hers which is included in my book, *A Modern Jew in Search of Soul*). I wish that she, like H. Rider Haggard, could get some value out of continuing to be "known," if only in the psyche of another appreciative writer. All serious writers, living and dead, as Haggard said, serve the Muse in one form or another, since the psyche itself is eternal.

The early 1970s, my forty-fifth until my fiftieth year, were surely a period of "nigredo" for me, the darkness spoken of by alchemist and mystics. The subsequent "albedo" and "rubedo," whitening and reddening, also took place, I hasten to assure other frustrated writers, and my "harvest time" has grown in earnest since my middle fifties, expressing the many-colored "peacock's tail." Astrologers speak of the first twenty-eight years of life as times of growing up, taking up a profession, marrying and beginning a family. So it was for me. They also speak of the second twenty-eight as a time of enhancing one's being, fulfilling one's destiny, suffering one's Self, so to speak. So it was for me. The third twenty-eight, beginning at age 56, is the time of harvest, and so it seems for me, too. I am glad I could conform with that pattern, but I do wish I could have known about it in advance, as it would have softened the suffering! But that is the point, perhaps. If I had not had the suffering, I could not have written the present book and its sister. The reader will have to decide for himself/herself if it was worth it. In "serene" retrospect, I think so.

Next, I want to thank my good friend, Gilbert Phelps, Fellow of the Royal Society of Literature, for adding his support, as did Henry Miller, to this peculiar kind of literature. The encouragement by a "real" writer, like Phelps (I am just a psychologist who also writes), has been of inestimable value. In the many years that I have known him, I have been impressed with his own dauntless courage in the face of the vicissitudes and rejections that come to most writers, even one such as he who has enjoyed great literary success with both critics and the public. But that mutual experience of friendship in the midst of worldly rejection will, I hope, itself be part of another book, jointly written, to appear in the future.

Finally, I want to thank Christopher S. Hyatt, Ph.D. my publisher, for risking the publishing of my work when it had such a dismal previous record. That all my subsequent books have "panned out," to use the gold-miner's apt expression, is a fitting reward for us both.

J. Marvin Spiegelman
Studio City, California
Summer 1990

POSTSCRIPT

The foregoing introduction was written in the belief that this book would soon appear. As one might have expected, given the obstructive history, a significant delay transpired. It is now some six years later, a quarter of century since *The Unpublished Writer* was first begun. A couple of years ago, my dear friend Gilbert Phelps died, and we were not able to actualize the join work that we had planned. He did, however, at my suggestion, write his "Confessions of a Failed Writer" before he died which I hope will be published one day. That an author such as he, who enjoyed both popular and critical success, could harbor such feelings might be consoling to the many writers who may be attracted to the theme of this book.

JMS, Fall 1996

Henry Miller, author of *Tropic of Cancer* has said of Dr. Spiegelman's work:

"For me, it was like sailing down a stream whose shores and everything bordering them was as familiar to me as if I had dreamt it a thousand times. I say familiar, but not stale. Rather like encountering in your sleep old dreams which you knew by heart but had not dreamt for many and many a year. Therefore extremely vivid and exciting. Or I could put it another way and say it was like presenting the quintessence of all one's spiritual experiences."

ACTIVE IMAGINATION AND STORY-WRITING: INDIVIDUATION AND ART
A chapter from *Jungian Psychology and The Passions of the Soul*
New Falcon Publications, First Edition, 1989

Ladies and Gentlemen:

Tonight I wish to speak to you about my own brand of psychological fiction or Jungian-influenced story-writing which I call–not too inflatedly, I hope–psycho-mythology." I shall speak about its origins, mythological connections, possible significance, and relation to both the process of individuation and artistic creativity. I also will both raise questions and attempt to answer them, hoping that you will bring up additional considerations at the end. Before I discuss "psycho-mythology," however, I must review the technique discovered or invented by Jung–namely, active imagination–out of which my own writing emerged.

Active Imagination, you may recall, was the method of exploring the unconscious that Jung happened upon in those days of floundering and isolation when he broke with Freud. Having completed the *"Symbole Der Wandlung"* and discovering the mythic basis of psychological contents–which led to his separation from Freud–he was left wondering what his own myth was, believing that he had none. He decided to let the psyche speak to him directly, without any prodding on his part. He began by playing with blocks and sand, just as he had as a child, building a little village and, in point of fact, originating what later came to be called "sand-play." In his autobiography, *Memories, Dreams,*

Reflections, he describes in a most human and exciting way his "confrontation with the unconscious," in which he gradually began to have dialogues with figures which emerged out of dream and fantasy. In his creative genius, he not only painted pictures and expressed the images which assaulted and engulfed him, he had the brilliant idea to actively relate to these figures, to communicate with them, confront them, treat them as if they were as real as anything in the outer world.

The years of such powerful inner conversation gave Jung the material for a lifetime of scientific investigation and reflection. This discovery of psychic reality not only gave him an understanding of the soul, but also provided a method that he could pass on to others whereby they, too, could investigate and experience the unconscious in their own souls. Armed with this technique, any one of us can embark upon a voyage of self-discovery. In so doing, we became both scientists and artists of the psyche and can either corroborate or disagree with what Jung, himself, experienced.

This method of active imagination held a central place for Jung, as one might guess. In both his *Letters* and as reported by Barbara Hannah (in *Active Imagination: Encounters with the Soul*), Jung said that the technique was absolutely crucial for anyone who wanted to become his own analyst, that it was the best way to become psychologically independent. As I have written elsewhere, ("Potentials of Active Imagination: Five Years Later" in *The Nymphomaniac*, Falcon Press, Phoenix, 1986), the method seems to be used rather less these days in analytical work, but many analysts swear by it for their own growth and emotional health.

And so it was for me, almost from the outset of my own analytical work as a patient. Within three months of the beginning of my first analysis in my mid-twenties, I made frequent use of the method. In my later training-analysis in Zürich, the method was a major source of both my psychological material and my active encounter with my own soul. This continued upon my return to the United States, after I completed my training, and provided both solace and understanding in the vagaries of existence that all analysts face. From 1950, then, until 1966, minus the two years during which I was a U.S. Army psychologist during the Korean War, active imagination and I were faithful friends.

Just after Christmas in 1966, I was also so engaged, but reflecting, too, on the year's events, which had seen my resignation from my local analytic society. For six months, I had been involved in a fantasy taking place in a cave. In that cave were a Mother and Daughter, a man of ancient age, and a young boy who could not speak. As I continued my dialogue with that Mother and Daughter, a large Knight appeared. He was dressed in black but had a golden sun emblazoned on his chest-plate. I recognized him from a dream I had had some months before. In that dream, the Knight and I were on a field of battle, perhaps in Macedonia. He looked strong, but battle-scarred and weary. As he gazed at me, he smiled wanly. I realized, in the dream, that he and I had both been engaged in the service of Jungian psychology in the outer world, and that was now going to end. I felt saddened but relieved by the dream, in that my decision to resign seemed to be confirmed by the unconscious. Now, many months later, this Knight was returning. Not only was he back, but now was carrying my friends, the Mother and Daughter, off on his horse. I was startled but, in my active imagination, I ran after him.

After I caught up with him, I asked him why he did that. He replied that he was just trying to get my attention. I told him that he certainly had it now, and he then made a surprising proposal. He told me that he, and also some others in his world, had stories to tell. Would I join them in writing these tales? I was not to be a mere amanuensis in this work, just take dictation. No. I was expected to participate and to contribute my own reactions and reflections, as well. We were to participate in this process together as a mutual endeavor. These stories, furthermore, were not only for own edification and enjoyment, but were intended for a larger public.

Although I was startled by this proposal from the Knight, as I have said, I was also excited by it. I had written stories in my adolescence, and even when I was a child, a favorite aunt had taken down a story of mine in dictation. For a time, I had thought to become a journalist, had even written a book about my experiences as a sailor in the Merchant Marine. I had doubts, however, about my skill or capacity as a writer. When I completed my sailor's book at age twenty, I hoped that it if it was published, I would go back to sea, write travel and short stories until I was forty, at which time I might be mature enough or deep enough to write novels. When the book was not accepted for publication, I decided to find some other career and gradually decided on psychology. So, here I was now, many years later in 1966, faced with the prospect of writing stories once more. But now I was, indeed, the very age of forty that I had magically selected for such work when I was twenty!

Not only did the story-writing desire of my youth once again come up for consideration, but I also remembered two other occasions in which this Knight-theme had appeared powerfully in my life. The first time was when I was less than four years old, just before my family moved from East Los Angeles to the West Adams district. I had been seated on my little tricycle, on the sidewalk in front of my parent's home on Sheridan Street. I remember awakening from a deep dream or fantasy, and not knowing what it was that I dreamt or imagined, but feeling its impact. Then I felt the power and warmth of the sun, directly above me. In the way that a child of three can understand such things, I felt that the sun was connected with God. But then I had the feeling that such a golden sun was also at my chest inside. I was bemused by there being a sun above in the sky and a sun within me. I was also struck by the words "sun" and "son" and felt myself in some way a "son of the sun." In all this, I felt quite special and very competent on my little tricycle, able to steer it here and there quite well.

In the midst of this sense of power and well-being, however I looked back at the house and was aware of my mother's presence there. As light and warm were the sun, as dark and uncertain were the house and my mother. Next door, also, there lived two little girls, one of whom was my friend, but the other one had scratched and hurt me. She, too, was dark and uncertain. So, there I was, at age three, faced with the problem of the opposites of sun and moon, light and dark, masculine and feminine, the three (tricycle) and the two (mother and little girl). Not that I understood anything of this at age three, of course, but I now realized, at age forty, that the Knight made his first appearance then. He also made me aware of the opposites, with my poor mother and the little girl as ripe object for my projects. I had to wait for middle life, however, to find out what this Knight was all about.

The second appearance of the Knight–or his representatives– occurred twenty-two years later, when I was twenty-five. It was the summer of 1951 and I was living a kind of monk's life. I had completed my job as a teaching assistant in the psychology department of UCLA graduate school, and was preparing to start my clinical internship with the Veterans Administration. I had also temporarily taken time off from analysis and was happily spending some weeks totally alone in my little one-room house over a garage on Chrysanthemum Lane in Beverly Glen. After several rather prescient dreams, I one night dreamed as follows:

> I was travelling around the world as a sailor with Marco Polo when suddenly a whirlwind comes up and envelopes me. It thrusts me into the Underworld where I meet the poet Virgil, who now accompanies me on adventures. The most significant

of these is an encounter with a large green dragon who spits red and yellow fire. I battle this dragon and succeed in overcoming it. Exhausted, I find myself alone on a kind of medieval street, but now, rather than in brilliant color, the dream continues in greys, black and white. I wander, weakened and alone, when suddenly a door on this street opens up and two huge Knights, dressed in green but with golden suns on their chests, grab me and bring me inside to a large circular arena, brilliantly lighted with intense color. The two Knights then proceed to beat me with branches from a tree, but as in a ritual, not with violence. After the beating, with branches from a tree, but as in a ritual, not with violence. After the beating, I see a crowd of people, among whom are a handsome French couple, and my professor and employer, Dr. Bruno Klopfer. They all look expectantly at me and then all eyes are turned towards a huge crown, shimmering with diamonds and other precious stones. The crown is of great beauty and majesty and I am enthralled by it, until I realize that I am about to be crowned. I see that this crown is far too large for me and I take a step back, overwhelmed with the prospect. As I retreat, the pleasure and anticipation of the crown turns to sorrow. I hear them say, in alternating sentences, as if undecided: "He is unworthy," or "He is too young." I awaken sobbing and with the realization that there are levels of the psyche far deeper and greater than anything that I had yet encountered and, indeed, far more serious than most things in the daylight world.

When I had written down this powerful dream, I remembered the event of my early childhood, but the true significance of all this had to await the reappearance of the Knight, in both dream and fantasy, when I was forty. Suffice it to say that this hero myth faced me at three and at twenty-five, but I was only ready to take it on consciously at the age of forty. The Crown of the Self, of course, was too big for me earlier on and, in some ways, it is too big for me even now. The personal part of the Self, as symbolized by the Crown, is to be found as the highest Sephira in the Kabbalah in Jewish mysticism, and is, at the same time, the highest chakra in the Kundalini Yoga of Hinduism. As such, it refers to that SELF, the God of us all, that Christmas Humphreys is talking about when he contrasts the self (or ego), with the Self (or personal authority) and the SELF (or transcendent, all-inclusive totality) [in Haifetz, *Zen and Hassidism*].

It is also not by chance that this Crown symbolism, so important in Kabbalah; should appear in this dream. My very first active imagination did not contain a crown but connected me quite shakingly with the *Zohar*, that central text in Jewish Kabbalistic mysticism, in a startling way. I had completed a written fantasy, along with some paintings, all of which I called, "Purple in the Blue." When I came to the waiting room of my analyst, Dr. Max Zeller, I found there, resting on the table, the five volumes of the *Zohar*, in English translation. They had just arrived, it seems. I had only heard of the name *Zohar* and knew nothing else about it. I picked up a volume at random and opened it somewhere in the middle. To my astonishment, I read therein a fantasy which was remarkably similar to the one I had just written! I walked up to Dr. Zeller's office trembling with this experience of synchronicity. So, one can see that the level from which the Knight came was indeed most powerful and deep.

To return, now, to my conversation with the Knight after Christmas 1966: I was in connection with all that happened many years before and was once again faced with the possibility of continuing this relationship, but in a more equal fashion. I therefore consented to do the writing work with the Knight and his friends, provided that this could be limited to two days per week. After all, I had a wife, children, and an analytic practice to attend to. Luckily for the project, I had just ended my seven-year teaching position at UCLA. So then, my story-writing began.

The Knight's tale was followed by that of an Arab whose theme was the struggle with passion and love. This tale drew somewhat on my experiences as a sailor travelling the world, particularly Egypt and

India, but the theme took place in the context of Muslim or Sufi piety and one result was a mandala with a crescent moon and star.

The third tale was Buddhistic and was based on the Zen Ox-Herding pictures. The hero, a Japanese Ronin, or samurai without a lord, pursued his adventures and enlightenment in close conjunction with the images and poems of that strikingly impactful series. All three of these men were clearly part of the hero myth, and each experienced this in connection with the individual process.

Following the three heroes, there appeared several women in sequence. Indeed, the remainder of the tales of women–five in number and equal to those of the men–constituted stage in what Jung referred to as the development of the feminine in a man, the ANIMA. The first woman's story was that of "Julia, the Atheist-Communist," who struggled with the problem of coming to be a mother, on the one hand, and with her atheism, on the other. The second woman's story was that of "Sybilla, the Nymphomaniac." Her's, a pagan tale, was the transformation of prostitute into bride of God and prophetess. "Maria, the Nun," was the third tale, that of a modern Catholic woman's engagement with the image of God.

After three women's tales, those of men resumed, alternating with the remaining women. First, was that of The African, which was a story of an American black man finding his spiritual roots in an alchemical work with an Abyssinian woman. This was followed by the story of May, the Yogini, a Hindu woman who pursued Kundalini Yoga in what one might call a feminist fashion. Then came the story of an Old Chinese Man who had an ongoing dialogue with Taoism and the *I Ching*, and finally, the Medium–Sophie-Sarah, who addressed the horrors of the Holocaust, using Kabbalistic knowledge. There were ten stories in all, along with poems by each seeker. The five women represented the five stages of anima development, as I have said, and, along with the five men, ten different religions, attitudes, or belief-systems were explored. All were individuation stories, all met at the Tree of Life in Paradise, and all found their own symbols fruitfully growing thereon. That book, therefore, was called *The Tree: Tales in Psycho-Mythology*.

Hardly had I completed that first book, however, when there appeared a young man calling himself the Son of the Knight. He wanted to continue the story-telling in a new book. He, it turned out, was from that original fantasy of the silent boy, old man, mother and daughter in the cave. The story be began proved to be also one of individuation, but now, in contrast to The Tree, the stories were in pairs. The first part of the book, for example, was that of the Son of the Knight and his companion, Dog. The second part was that of Mother and Daughter. The Son of the Knight story also contained a hero quest in it, although somewhat different from the usual myth. The tale of Mother and Daughter included the Demeter-Persephone theme in the background but also had Christian aspects to it. The third part of the book shifted form dyads to triads. A tale of King Arthur, Queen Guinevere, and Sir Lancelot was involved, and the whole book was rounded out in a search after the Grail. This second book was called *The Quest: Further Tales in Psycho-Mythology*.

Confident of what the Knight had told me in the first place—that the work was meant for a larger public than myself—and also buoyed up by the positive response to it from my friend, the author Henry Miller, and the support of Anais Nin, I sent the first book out to various publishers. After several years and about forty rejections, I thought that there might be some mistake—either in the Knight's predictive capacity or his assessment of my skill or in the receptivity of the times.

At last, however, a small publisher was found for *The Tree*. This publisher, alas, went bankrupt—not, I hasten to add, because of my book, since the thousand printed copies did sell out. At that point, I resumed my writing, but the title of my next work became *The Failures*. The heroes of that work, if one can call them that, were an *Unpublished Writer*, an *Unhealed Healer*, and *Empty Teacher*, and an *Unfrocked Priest*! They all met at the mountain retreat of the Powerless Magician. That book almost ended in failure, of course, but after a time there was a sequel to it, called *The Successes*, in which that same set of people continued their exploration in another way. In the meantime, another publisher had appeared. He reprinted *The Tree* in 1982, and published *The Quest* in 1984. He has also encouraged my non-fiction work, which has been appearing in book form.

Well, then, that is the story of my stories. What does it all mean? It is, itself, a kind of hero–or even anti-hero–myth of myself? Yes, I think so. But I believe there is more to it, and we will now try to address what this might mean.

Jung, you will recall, made a strict distinction between active imagination and art. The former was aimed at the creation of the personality rather than towards work of art. One must clearly find a balance between the need for understanding and the aesthetic need in such an endeavor. In his *Memoirs*, Jung tells us how he was tempted by a siren feminine voice, both inner and outer, who told him that his work was "art." He manfully resisted that insinuation and persuaded himself–and us–that his work was in the interest of science. What was needed was for the person to understand and transform himself, not just be a mouthpiece for the unconscious which, perhaps, many artists became.

That Jung took his tack is certainly a good thing for the rest of us. Many of his discoveries came from this work. Nor does his writing–for instance, the *Sermones Ad Mortuous*–seem particularly artistic, although some of his paintings are quite impressive. This is the case with most products of active imagination, as we know. They may have some artistic merit, but they are clearly expressive of the individual psyche rather than works of art.

How, then, do I view my own story-writing? Is it, perhaps, failed art or active imagination misunderstood? I think not. First of all, I did regular active imagination for sixteen years before even beginning that kind of story-writing. Secondly, the material which appears, as I have said, is in the form of tales by figures from the unconscious. If it is active imagination, it is done by the archetypal figures themselves. This, I think, brings it beyond the personal level to a transpersonal one. Thirdly, whether or not it is art remains to be determined by time and criticism. The stories need to walk about on their own legs and see if they can manage in that literary world and effort people. I hope and believe that they can. They certainly have had something of an impact so far, but to what extent they will do so remains to be seen.

I originally described this kind of work, wherein a Jungian Analyst was writing mythological stories, as a new genre, "psycho-mythology." I hope that this is not an inflationary neologism. It just seemed to me that a newer kind of art was in the making, something like science-fiction or the historical novel. In the latter two genres, there is an amalgamation of imagination with either scientific facts and theories, or with historical knowledge. In psycho-mythology, I thought, there was a union, in story form, between psychological knowledge and imagination.

There has been other psychological fiction, of course, but has there been fiction influenced by Jung's discoveries? And fiction which would directly touch on the mythological level of psyche? Not to my knowledge. In the years from 1967 to the 70s, there was not the interest in Jung that there is now, and there were no colleagues of mine, as far as I know, who were so engaged. I still do not know of any, but someone has recently called my attention to essays by Ursula Le Guin, a science-fiction writer, which shows a very good understanding, indeed, of Jungian psychology. (Le Guin, Ursula. *The Language of the Night*. G.P. Putnam's Sons,

New York, 1979, 270 pp.) I have not yet read any of her fictional work, so I can not say to what extent she is working in roughly the same area that I am. So, one does not yet know whether there is really a new genre or not, or even the extent to which Jung's work and particularly his invention/discover of active imagination will have an effect on the literary/artistic mind.

I have to ask myself, however, how do I understand the writing I have done, psychologically? That it is clearly part of my own myth and individuation process goes without saying. One might even claim, with fairness, that the work IS my myth. I would not quarrel with this conclusion, but I would add that parts of my myth are not included in it, that other myths are, and that the myth is continuing. I would also agree that the contents can be interpreted. In much of the writing, however, the psychological view-point, including interpretation, is included in it. I would even go so far as to say that part of the claim and an implied criticism. Some psychological interpretation of artistic work or writing seems reductive and destructive to me: the critic stands apart and comments or fires barbs at the creative person. In the case of psycho-mythology, however, interpretation–rather than being above and apart–is part of the art itself. If the interpretation is not part of the art and does not advance the process, it is useless, if not destructive. In short, interpretation serves the art, rather than the reverse, and I think this is valuable. The foregoing is one form of psychological understanding of psycho-mythology.

Another way to understand what I am doing in such writing, I found in that branch of Jewish mysticism and magical work called Kabbalah. It comes, of course, from the central image of that field, THE TREE OF LIFE. That tree, you will recall, encompasses tenfold aspects of the divine, just as the Trinity encompasses threefold aspects. In the center of The Tree, half way up–for those who "climb" The Tree in their apprehension of and relationship with

God—is the Sephira (as it is called), of Tiphereth. This is the androgynous God-Man-Woman position on the Tree, and also that of Beauty and Art. The seeker comes up from his mortal Tree, and also that of Beauty and Art. The seeker comes up from his mortal existence to it. One could just as easily say "down," since The Tree of Life has its roots in heaven and grows downward towards us.

At Tiphereth, one experiences a union of the divine and the human. I would say that each of the hero-figures of my books are indeed both divine and mortal, or seen psychologically, are both archetypal and personal. I myself climb up to them and when they, in turn, are having experiences, they are in touch with higher or deeper qualities of the divine principle itself. This, it seems to me, is an imaginal representation of Jungian psychology itself. In analytical psychology, we are constantly apprehending the archetypal, but we come to it via the personal experience of ourselves or with people with whom we work. The claim of psycho-mythology is that the archetypal transcends the personal in this kind of writing, and it may be, therefore, of more general interest or value. Such was the view of the Knight, his friends and heirs, and such is my view, too. Whether you agree or not, is for you to say.

An Introduction to
THE TREE OF LIFE
Paths In Jungian Individuation
New Falcon Publications, Second Edition, 1993

It is more than a quarter of a century since I began to write *The Tree of Life: Paths in Jungian Individuation* (originally published as *The Tree*). Much has changed since that Knight came into my psyche and into my active imagination, announcing that he and others like him had stories to tell, both for me and for others. I am writing this new introduction, however, on that same Hermes portable that I used then (bought when I was a student at the C.G. Jung Institute in Zürich from 1956-1959–even though I now have a Macintosh word-process. Maybe, nostalgia, maybe honoring the Knight. This, the third printing of the book, allows not only errors to be corrected (and new ones to come in!), but also permits me to say a few words about how that exciting invention of "psychomythology–as I called it then–has fared.

I thought, then, that this union of psychological fact and fiction, reaching the mythological level of the soul, would introduce a new genre to literature, like science fiction and the historical novel. Well, so far, aside from my own work, I do not think it has. I produced two more works in that trilogy, *The Quest* and *Jungian Psychology and the Passions of the Soul* (originally titled *The Love*), and am, even now, engaged in another such union of fact and fancy, called *Failures and Successes*, but no one else has taken up this challenge to combine what we have learned from Jungian psychology with the arts—at least, I should add, the way it came to me! Indeed, I have been privileged to have, as analysands, several artists, particularly film and television writers, who have indeed combined their inner process and exploration with their creativity as artists to produce works of considerable value and depth.

Perhaps that is as it should be. The Freudian psychoanalytic exploration of art and the artist mined that field rather thoroughly in the 20s to the 50s. That approach no longer has much appeal. The particular diagnostic, reductive attitude had about as much value, culturally speaking, as the various diagnoses of van Gogh, namely minimal. None of them touched the mystery, for example, of "Vincent's" spiritual quest. Yet such examination of our historical heroes (even of Washington's wooden teeth) does excite our interest.

I think it more useful to do what my analysands and others have done—namely to use their psychological knowledge and experience to deepen their own creative work. If that helps produce more satisfying and enlightening art, all the better. Depth psychology, like Reason for Plato, is best in the service of the passions (their "slave", as he put it), with regard to art, rather than being used in some questionable diagnostic fashion. Even in analysis, few analysts really pay much attention to the DSM III or IV categories which are of central issue to the insurance companies.

Readers have told me—and I agree with them—that *The Tree of Life* has given them at least two kinds of insight. The first has been a vivid description of the individuation process as Jung has discussed it, but in a colorful and expressive fashion which is not revealed in theoretical or clinical presentations. Secondly, these readers have told me that reading these stories brings a kind of enlightenment about various religions and spiritual paths such as Gnosticism (The Knight), Buddhism (The Ronin), Hinduism and Kundalini (Maya, The Yogini), Kabbalah (The Medium, Sophie-

Sarah), and so forth. I am most pleased that the stories have had this effect. I am also glad that others have written to say that they have just enjoyed the book.

And so the reader has in his/her hands a labor of love and inspiration that has stood up for this quarter-century as many other things have not. The letters that I have received over the years lead me to believe that those who have been touched by it, in the service of their own development, are the true answer to The Knight's instruction to me (echoed by the other seekers in the book, belonging to different religions and non-religions), "Let each know where the other is!"

J. Marvin Spiegelman, Ph.D.
Studio City, California
Spring, 1993

PSYCHO-MYTHOLOGY
A New Literary Genre
A chapter from *The Tree of Life: Paths In Jungian Individuation*
New Falcon Publications, Second Edition, 1993

> "Active fantasy being the principal attribute of the artistic mentality, the artist is not merely *representer*, he is also a *creator*, hence essentially an educator since his works have a value of symbols that trace out the line of future development. Whether the actual social validity of the symbol is more general or more restricted depends upon the quality or vital capacity of the creative individuality." —C.G. Jung, Psychological Types (1, p.580 f)

With the term "psycho-mythology," I wish to introduce a new literary genre which bears a familial resemblance to both science-fiction and the historical novel. In these forms, there is a peculiar kind of union of the opposites of fact and fiction. Science fiction starts with current scientific knowledge, makes reasonable extrapolations towards future discoveries, and fuses these with fantasy. Historical novels add romance, conjectured conversation and embellishment to what is known of recorded events. In both cases, the structure of "truth" and "reality" is enriched by imagination, which is psychological truth.

"Psycho-mythology" stands for a similar union of fact and imagination, but in this field there is a marriage of psychological knowledge with the type of fantasy that reaches the universal, archetypal, mythological level. I am not referring to the well-known psychological novel, which uses the insights of psychology to probe the depths of a particular personality. That form is closer to the genre of the detective story or the clinical case study, although it can reach heights of artistic excellence as, for example, in Dostoievsky's *Crime and Punishment*.

Rather than concerning itself with the motivations of an individual, psycho-mythology relates to the collective psyche and its drama. Paradoxically, the perturbations of the modern man, occupied with his struggle for individuation, is both the source and core of it. The reason for this is that the invention or discovery of this genre came out of sixteen years of experience of C.G. Jung's "Active Imagination" (2).

Psycho-mythology is a literature in which an individual's fantasy transcends the personal level, reaching the collective unconscious. In addition, the work is consciously connected with either available religious or mythical material and is clearly intended as a work of art. With this definition, the genre is seen to straddle both what has been customarily called Active Imagination, as taught by Jung, and Art. In active imagination, the intention is a confrontation by the individual with the unconscious, with the aim of expanding his consciousness and fostering individuation and wholeness. In art, any development of consciousness or wholeness is to produce an esthetically satisfying work, which may communicate some quality or experience to others, or may be for itself alone. In art, any development of consciousness or wholeness in the artist is largely incidental. Indeed, there are those who claim that the intrusion of psychological knowledge, aims, or attitude is hurtful to the art or the artist. For psycho-mythology, I shall claim, there is a fusion of the psychological need for growth of consciousness, with the artistic need of esthetics, communication, and for its own sake.

Before I relate how I came to discover or create this genre, I would like to say a few more words about Jung and active imagination. As is well-known to all who have read Jung's wonderful and remarkable autobiography, *Memories, Dreams and Reflections* (3), the great psychologist discovered the method of confrontation with the unconscious after he had broken with Freud. At this time, he was isolated, did not know his direction, and was convinced that the had no personal myth at all. He began to play with his fantasy and with the figures who emerged in that play and from his dreams. He was the first to take the products of that play seriously and to relate to the dwellers of the unconscious as if they were as real as any Swiss Burgher that one might meet strolling the Limat in Zürich. He realized that these figures, though autonomous, were products of his own soul and he undertook a relationship with them.

In this process, Jung changed both the unconscious and himself. Greatly moved by this activity, which lasted several years in his late thirties, he made most of the discoveries which were to be developed during the remainder of his life. The importance of Active Imagination, therefore, was as central for Jung as was the focus upon dreams. Yet he was reluctant to publish very much on this topic. He did produce some work in this area (1, 2) and others are now following upon this beginning (6).

Jung's reluctance in publishing on the topic of Active Imagination was strange since he thought this method would ultimately free an individual from dependence upon any analyst at all! He says this beautifully in his Letters (4, pp. 458-461). He recognized that the work of Active Imagination contained both the need for Understanding (which was the effort to raise consciousness) and the Aesthetic (for beautiful and satisfying expression). In his earliest work on the topic (2), he clearly perceived that the method would lead now one way and now the other, yet he was adamant in asserting that this material was surely not art, but had a psychological aim.

The reason for Jung's assertion, in my opinion, comes from his experience of the female personage (whether a fantasy "anima" person or a real, living one) mentioned in his autobiography (3). That lady, when shown the beautiful paintings and writings of the artist-poet that Jung was, said that he should be and was an artist. Jung hotly denied this, saying that he was a scientist! I think that Jung struggling to keep his psychological discoveries in the realm of science had to lean over backwards and even sacrifice the true artistic value of some of what he produced. Those who have seen some of the paintings of the Red Book in the film of Jung, or read the poetry of his "Sermons of the Dead" (5), already know his artistic capacity. Furthermore, those of us who follow Jung appreciate the scientific value of his discoveries, no longer need to keep the method of Active Imagination strictly in the psychological workbasket, and can allow its expansion in other ways.

Another hindrance to Active Imagination becoming better known lies not with Jung alone, but also with some of his followers. There are those who are fearful of speaking about it, believing it to be a tool of the second half of life alone, and a dangerous one at last, properly limited to those who are supervised in analysis (6). I am less fearful, having discovered that the technique is difficult for most people to embark upon, quite demanding of discipline and commitment to stay with, thus outside the grasp of the merely dilettante. As for possible danger, the psyche seems to have its natural protections of boredom, fear, skepticism, or inflation, all of which dissuade the non-devoted. I would add that from the artistic standpoint, probably even fewer of those who embark upon this work will produce material which, as Jung has said, will "communicate with the past and with the future, as well as with contemporaries (1,pp. 5 75 f).

A further consideration of Active Imagination can be found in the references. At this point, I wish to tell the story of how I happened upon "psycho-mythology". But, before I do, I feel the necessity of mentioning other available examples of the field.

Strictly speaking, there are none, since the method has grown out of Jung's discoveries and his psychology, so that only the future will produce such works of art. Yet there are forerunners, I think, such as Goethe's Faust, or Thomas Mann's Holy Sinner, to mention only very great ones. These works, on can see, meet the definition of carrying religious-mythological significance, are psychologically insightful, reach the collective psyche, as well as intending artistic expression. The also carry both individual and collective significance simultaneously. Perhaps you can think of other examples.

Now to the story of my stories. On December 28, 1966, I was seated at my desk in my office, reflecting upon the preceding year's events, which had been painful, momentous and shattering for me. During that year, I had found it necessary to resign from my local professional analytic society and to break off some relationships which had proved to be illusory. That day, I was engaged in active imagination, which had been my custom at least twice a week for many years. I had started his process just a few months after beginning my own analysis in 1950 and had continued with it, with only a two year interruption during military service, ever since. It had proved to be especially valuable when I ceased working with any analyst at all some three years previous.

The particular fantasy I had been working on for some months involved being in a cave with an old man, a woman and her daughter, and a young boy with dark eyes who did not speak. I was talking with the group when suddenly a huge Knight, wearing black armor with a golden sun emblazoned on his breastplate, broke in abducted the mother and daughter, riding away on his horse. I recognized this Knight from a dream I had had some six months earlier. In that dream, which took place after I resigned from the professional society, this Knight appeared and said to me that he had been at my side for a long time, but that now we no longer had a cause to serve. I understood him to mean the collective Jungian cause, as it worked as an institution in the world. I was aware, also, that the Knight was representative of my own inner "hero" figure, going back to early childhood. At the age of three, for example, I had a powerful experience of sitting on my tricycle and feeling the power of God high above and warming me from the sun, and also located inwardly, as an equal power, at my chest.

Now this dream hero appeared in earnest and was carrying off two important feminine figures. I pursued him, continuing my fantasy, and asked him why he did that and what he wanted. The Knight replied that he abducted those ladies in order to get my full attention and that he had some stories to tell. Would I be interested in hearing them, he wondered! He also hinted that there were other people there who had tales to tell, should I be inclined to take the time to hear them and work with them. He suggested that these stories were important for others to hear, as well as for myself. Excitedly, but somewhat skeptically, I agreed to attend to these tales, provided the work could be kept with the periods I had available for such activity. After all, I had patients, family, and other demands upon my time. He agreed, and then began a work which was to take most of two days per week for several years. The Knight's tale was followed by that of a Moslem Arab, a Japanese Buddhist Ronin, and then by three women; Julia, the Athiest-Communist, Sybilla, the Nymphomaniac, and Maria, the Nun. Thereafter came stories by the African, which was alchemical in nature, Maya, the Yogini who performed a kind of Kundalini Yoga, the tale of the Old Chinese Man who struggled with the spirit of the *I Ching*, and finally the Medium, the woman named Sophie-Sarah who embraced Kabbalah.

These ten people each told a story of their own individuation, and each represented a different religion or syncretism, or some meditative, consciousness-seeking activity. Each was rather unorthodox, yet all found themselves at the Tree of Life. Altogether, their tales constituted what came to be called *The Tree*.

This series, some six hundred typewritten pages in length, was barely completed when there appeared another person, who called himself the Son of the Knight. This chap pursued a different series of myths, and this second book took up his quest, and also that of a Mother and Daughter in a cave, a part of the Grail legend involving King Arthur, Lancelot, and Queen Guinevere. That four-hundred page book was called *The Quest*.

I must add that I was no mere amaneusis to these storytellers. I often found myself not only relating their tales, but also living them and identifying with them as each of them approached the Gods. I worked and learned with them, although my true ego place seems to be somewhere else, more like the present narrator, but also as multiple and various as all of these, my deep inner friends. It remains for our mutual work to go out to the world and walk among men. "Let each know where the other is," was the message to the Knight, and so say I, too.

REFERENCES

1. Jung, C.G. *Psychological Types*. Routledge and Kegan Paul, London, 1923. Also Collected Works, Vol. 6.
2. Jung, C.G. *The Transcendent Function*, orig. 1916, published in Collected Works, Vol. 8.
3. Jung, C.G. *Memories, Dreams, Reflections*. Pantheon Books, New York, 1961.
4. Jung, C.G. *Letters,* Vol. 1: 1906-1950. Princeton University Press, 1973.
5. Jung, C.G. *VII Sermones ad Mortuos*. Stuart and Watkins, London, 1961, Orig. 1925.
6. Weaver, Rix. *The Old Wise Woman, a Study of Active Imagination*. G.P. Putnam's Sons, New York 1973.

An Introduction to
THE QUEST
New Falcon Publications, First Edition, 2021

New Falcon Publications, booksellers and some others have told me that there is some question as to just what my books of fiction intend. My statement that they are just stories, and meant to be read that way does not suffice, since I am a psychologist and a Jungian Analyst and, indeed, my introduction to *The Tree* clearly affirmed that I thought of my work as "psycho-mythology," to blend a fiction and psychological fact, just as science-fiction or historical novels combine the knowledge of scholarly disciplines with story.

I stand guilty as charged, therefore, and feel obliged to give a fuller accounting of the trilogy of which *The Tree* was the first, I shall give some additional details in the matter. As some have intuited, there was, indeed, another structure and intention than is usually subsumed in a fictional work.

First of all, my "psycho-mythology" grew out of many years of use of Jung's method of "active imagination." This technique is described fully in the two essays which introduce my little book, *The Knight*, to which I respectfully direct those interested in origins. Here, let me suffice to say that the method is one of making conscious what people do all the time, namely talk to themselves. We are constantly engaged in a more-or-less conscious inner dialogue, talking or quarreling with ourselves, with friends and enemies, with loved ones and strangers. We also fantasize images and stories some of the time. It was Jung's genius to discover that one could consciously take up these barely aware quarrels and fantasies and pursue these "as-if" discussions with a measure of psychological reality. Such serious listening to our inner friend or antagonist, and sincerely continuing the relationship with a full measure of openness and commitment, ultimately leads to the discovery of all the archetypal figures of the psyche that Jung has written about–shadow, anima/animus, old wise man/woman, Self, etc. This need not be just ego chatter, but can be a true encounter with the larger personality, of which the ego is merely a part.

In the essays mentioned above, I noted that I had valuably used Jung's method of inner dialogue for some fourteen years when one day there was a quantum jump for me, in that the work was no longer merely for my own enlightenment and development, but suddenly took on the possibility of social usefulness. That, at least, was the opinion of an inner figure I was working with. Just after Christmas in 1966, a Knight–who had appeared in a dream many months before and had also made appearances in dreams and fantasies in early childhood and in my middle twenties–came forward and said that he had a story to tell, not just for my benefit but for others as well. There were additional people there in the background who also wanted to share their tales. The telling was to include me not just as amanuensis or transcriber, but as a participant in the work. I agreed to undertake this task, and spent the next four years, two days a week, engaged in the writing, thus producing these books. These were: *The Tree*, published in the first time in 1975 (eight years after its completion) and re-published in 1983; *The Quest*, published for the first time in 1984 (sixteen years after its completion);.

One might well ask why the publication of these books has taken such a long time, since these archetypal figures were of the impression that their stories would be of general interest and value.

I certainly wondered about it at the outset. The answers that have come center around the idea that the time was not yet ripe or that the stories were not good enough from one point-of-view or another. I am unable to judge this. Some worthy people (e.g. Henry Miller) thought the stories were quite good indeed, others that they were too difficult. This puzzles me since the language used is generally accessible to persons with average education. It is true that some of the tales (e.g. that of Maya, the Yogini), contain technical terms from various spiritual disciplines. All of the latter are defined, however, so that most people seem to understand them. The history of the publication of the stories is fraught with frustration and rejection, much like that of mythological hero tales of which *The Tree* and *The Quest* are examples. I must leave it to the reader to arrive at his own judgement. For my part, I would like these tales to walk about on their own feet and endure their fate. I am pleased to know that they do reach out here and there and find their proper audience. I am grateful for the letters I have received from readers who have been touched by them.

Before I go on to tell more about the structure and content of the stories, here is a capsule version of *The Tree* for those who may not be acquainted with that book.

THE STRUCTURE OF *THE TREE*

The organization of The Tree is of ten tales, told by five men and five women. Each story is of a heroic nature, though the people are quite ordinary, of this world. They come from different times, spiritual origins, beliefs and religions, but each is a tale of individuation, of a pursuit of wholeness and meaning based on their own experience of the divine. The first three stories are by men with no name, but rather they have a quality or character to them. The Knight is timeless, but partakes of Jewish, Christian, and pagan qualities and mirrors best the theme of the Gnostic search for an answer to the question of evil. The Arab, who follows him, adds the Islamic skein to the picture, and pursues in the outer world what the Knight sought within. But the inner is not lacking in the Arab's moon-consciousness as he seeks and finds a transformation of his own passion and greed into love. The Ronin, the third male in this nameless triad, has the Buddhist slant on things. As a Japanese Samurai warrior without a lord, his quest follows the sequence of the ten Ox-Herding pictures, so well-known in Zen, and his psyche finds its wholeness in that process.

The three tales of women which follow are more personal in one sense–they all have names–but are also archetypal. They are meant to be quite characteristic of women, but also come from the stages of development of the *anima* (the image of the feminine in the male psyche), as described by Jung. Julia, the Atheist-Communist, is Mother and struggles with the issue of motherhood and creativity, although her spiritual battle is political. Sybilla, the Nymphomaniac, is Hetaira (prostitute into priestess and oracle), who reconciles the warring gods within herself. Maria, the Nun, is a spiritual priestess as Sybilla was an earth priestess. She overcomes taboo and the flesh and brings a renewal of the Christian story into the modern day.

This sequence of three males and three females is followed by four tales in which masculine and feminine are more blended. First comes The African, who is now a man with a name, searching for the spiritual origins of his existence and happens upon the alchemistic route of transformation. Next is Maya the Yogini, who takes up her traditional Hindu religion in the form of Kundalini Yoga, but does so alone and with a guru who comes to her from within her own soul. The Old Chinese Man is truly eastern and Chinese, Taoist, and sheds light upon himself and his name, as well as the nature of his faith by dialogue with a book, the *I Ching*. Finally, The Medium, Sophie-Sarah, goes into the depths of the Kabbalistic mystery and tries to answer the impossible question of the suffering of her people. She, carrying the image of Wisdom, completes the five stages of anima development described by Jung, following the *femme inspiratrice* stage of Maya, the Yogini.

These ten, meeting at The Tree of Life in paradise, all conclude that the task of humankind, at the present stage of evolution, is to realize the divine within themselves, and to become conscious of their own individuality and particularity. They all learn that the divine needs the human being for its fulfillment, just as the human needs the divine.

THE STRUCTURE OF *THE QUEST*

Just as *The Tree* represented the heroic mode and the seeking of salvation on an individual level, The Quest carries on this search, but now the stories are in pairs and multiples and the whole book has the quality of a single tale, the parts more dovetailed with each other. Rather than a totality of ten, there are three parts here. The first section takes up the story of *The Knight* but in a second generation. Here the Son of the Knight goes out to find his origins, but does so in the company of a dog, his friend and co-seeker. Thus, the section is called *Son of the Knight and Dog*. The parts of the tale have chapter headings, and the story is more like the early English and Spanish novel in style. The content, however, is also one of learning and healing, in which the *Son of the Knight and Dog* go through similar experiences–initiation by women, for example–but from different points-of-view. Through their experiences, both are redeemed and make the discovery of the divinization of man and the humanization of the divine.

The second part of *The Quest* is that of *Mother and Daughter*. Again a pair-story is involved, with mutual individuation and redemption the result. It may be noticed that the classical story of Demeter and Persephone is the background of this tale, just as the hero myth provided background to that of the *Son of the Knight*. This tale of the development of the feminine was also influenced by the story of Ben Hur, it may be noticed by some. Tarot card themes also play a role.

The third part of *The Quest* not only shows the union and surprising connection of the first two parts, but now takes up the problem of multiple integration and union, of all the figures of the tales. The story copes with the theme of "threeness", just as the previous tales resolved the issues of "oneness" and "twoness." Here, therefore, King Arthur, Sir Lancelot and Queen Guinevere serve as models for the search for that Grail of wholeness. The union achieved in the book stands by itself, just as that of *The Tree* did.

Suffice it to say that these books can be read separately but also entail a development in which the archetypes are fleshed out in story form and provide a panoply of a modern myth. I have said, perhaps, too little or too much, but hope that this short introduction will give some answers to the question of what an analyst who writes fiction is up to. Essentially, what I am describing, in story form, is an adventure into the unconscious, from which the themes of origin, good and evil, love and self-realization are revealed as both personal and transpersonal events. But now let the Son of the Knight and his friends speak for themselves.

A CAPSULE OF *THE TREE*
A Psycho-Mythological Tale in Ten Parts
A chapter from *THE QUEST*
New Falcon Publications, First Edition, 2021

I, J. Marvin Spiegelman, Ph.D., Clinical Psychologist, Jungian Analyst, have taken an archetypal journey, an inward exploration. In the course of this adventure, I have met ten different people, of other times and places, of other races and religions, each of whom has told me a tale of his own inner journey. I dutifully and devotedly recorded the accounts of their experiences in a six-hundred page manuscript which, in turn, proved to be the first of three volumes.

These ten people (and I) are eager to have their stories known, but, in the busy pace of the modern day, it seems difficult to attract attention to such timeless tales. A friend has suggested that a capsule version of the first volume, *The Tree*, might entice a person to look at the whole. Not knowing how to reduce their stories myself, I have asked these ten people to do so themselves, and the following is what each has had to say.

THE KNIGHT

It is true that I am a Knight, albeit a rather peculiar one, for I am of the ancient time and the modern age; I am both Jewish and Christian and acknowledge a pagan soul, as well. From a youthful life of joy and carefree play with companions, I was summoned by an Angel of God to go on a great journey to different places on earth and in the sea. The reason for this journey was because God was dead or abandoned, or split in pieces, and needed human help. In truth, God was a humpty-dumpty and the world was in sore pain because of it. I, therefore, under the guidance of my Angel, found what seemed to be God or Devil, under the sea. There, beneath the waves, he was a wise man who told a strange tale of self-sacrifice. He had helped men, lived with them as their king, wanted to be their brother, head even given his son as a sacrifice for them. But men still thought that he was the source of the evil in their lives, so he retired under the sea. Knights came to kill him, but upon hearing the story, they embraced him. They either kept silent or went mad with the thought that what men thought was God was Devil, and the reverse; for all were trained to believe that this King was the source of evil. My encounter with this King was even more shaking, since I learned from the Angel that God did not know of his own Power which dwelt in heaven—he was split off from this other half of Himself? Thus, I was faced with a paradox: God was unconscious and lived in two places, each not knowing where the other was. He needed man to help redeem Him, my Angel said

Next I found God under the earth. He had been a benevolent brother under the sea, but under the earth he was a suffering mother. Here she felt every pain, knew every fallen leaf. I sat and silently shared all these pains until I, too, knew in my own soul God the Mother, the suffering God.

And then I came to that same Power in Heaven, which was so fearsome and judging and awe-full, the very Eye of God. And Him I saw on a mountain triangle in the desert. He it was who shook me with his wrath and fierce judgment of men. But I stood and was not destroyed, though I felt the paradox of God's complexity and his separation into parts. I endured God's split and there ensued a softening and warming; the fearful father became benevolent. I then realized that it was the rejected first Son of God, called snake and Devil, who was at fault.

So, I went to the snake—or, rather, the snake came to me. This Devil-Son spoke of creation and destruction, of God's dark moods creating deserts, his tears forming lakes. He spoke, too, of God's need of a partner in order to gain self-knowledge, and of how this first son was the carrier of the same. The Devil-Son questioned and insinuated, probed and criticized. Therefore was he the despised and loved one, the needed and rejected of God. I learned once more that what was known as evil was not so. I grasped that what truly was evil was the separation of the parts of God from each other, and the separation of God and man. With this realization, there came a great vision of the union of God the Father, God the Brother, and God the Son, in a great triangle, and I was relieved of my own division and gained some peace thereby.

But relief was brief. Once again I was summoned by the Angel. This time I faced, not God's maleness, but femaleness—beauty and poetry and love—in the form of God the Sister and God the Daughter. These I tasted and relished, but there then came God the Raging Mother, she who had been rejected, separated and far from God the wise. The female triangle returned with ferocity and rapine, as well as with love and beauty, and I knew what it meant to be raped by God.

At last the two triangles merged and made the Star of the People of David, and the Seal of the people of Solomon. I saw this sign upon a great Tree, whose roots went everywhere in the Earth and whose limbs reached all parts of the sky. And I saw that this tree contained all those symbols and signs of men's devotion and religion, of their belief and experience. It was the Angel who told me that this was the Tree of Life, kept apart from men since the early days by the flaming sword, but now open to him who could understand, "Ye are Gods." And I knew, and told my tale: God needs man.

THE ARAB

My story is a tale of love and passion, of pain and grief, of union and reconciliation. A man meant to be a healer, I fell in love, but violated my beloved. A simple matter: there was more passion and greed in me than love. So I fled and wandered the earth. As a sailor, I sailed the seas and saw all manner of men and manners. I fed the raging hyena within me to satisfy all the lusts revolted and submitted. And I learned. At last, in a temple of the great goddess Kali in India, I came to understand the animal and its sacrifice. I learned of the taming of passion by its feeding and endurance, by its sacrifice. I learned of the taming of passion by its feeding and endurance, by its sacrifice and submission, by its transformation into the pearl of great price, into the jewel of a thousand lights, into the star-sapphire which fell from the moon. And I brought this jewel to my beloved who had loved me and knew of my love when I did not. But she, grieving in loss of me and waiting too long, had since married my friend. We loved in the moment and I was healed and redeemed. In later days, I married another love, and became a healer in truth. It was then that I saw my own star and crescent upon that self-same Tree which carried the star of the Knight. And I heard this tale. Hearing of his quest, I told some tales to edify him, and then told my own. But best of all, I spoke of God. In some poems I spoke, and in the colorful tale of where and what with whom I had my voyages, and what it was that I learned about my passion. For I learned to love.

THE RONIN

My story is brief, since I am a Ronin, a warrior and a monk of Japan, who fights and mediates and speaks little. My tale, beginning with the injustices done to me by my masters, is told in words to the famous Zen drawings, the Ox-Herding pictures.

I sought the bull of my nature. I found it, I wrestled with it, I tamed it, alone and apart. But then, I came to love the bull of my soul. I played the flute upon its back and came home with it. I found myself and my own nature, which just is. Then once again I went to the mountain and meditated. I gave myself up, for it was the "me" which was the source of pain and suffering. And I vanished, for I knew that nature, the Tree, was the Source.

At last, I came back to the market place and told my tale and lived my life and gave of my blessings to others. Then it was that I came to the garden where both Knight and Arab were telling their tales under that great Tree of trees. Hearing their stories, I told my own which, though brief, was most moving to them. They embraced me and I, though it was strange for me, embraced them in return. There it is for all to hear, but I cannot repeat it, since life moves on. The lion roars, the sword glints, and Buddha is.

JULIA, THE ATHEIST-COMMUNIST

My story is several-sided: it is a record of the life of a Jewish girl born in Poland, raised in America, who chooses Israel; it is a tale of barrenness and depression in a modern woman who is uncreative and must go deeply into a quest for self-knowledge; it is a tale of generations; it is a story of how one becomes a psychologist; it is a portrait of the atheistic and communist mine, the how and why of it. Finally, it is a tale of how the great diversity becomes a unity in the mind and in life; it is a story of how sickle becomes psi, how one could become an atheist for God, a communist for man. The story was told in the garden to all the others by that same Tree.

SYBILLA, THE NYMPHOMANIAC

Mine, too, is a tale of passion. A daughter of Greek and Egyptian, of Christian and Moslem, I was born out of wedlock, out of grace, and out of time. Gods took me. Gods of Greece and Egypt. They came and possessed me, and from an early age, I was nymphomaniac. I suffered and sought, was degraded and destroyed–almost. Near death from pain and horror, I wandered into the great desert until I came to a cave and met the rabbi who cured me. He, rejected by his people and himself, accompanied me upon the voyage of confrontation of those Gods and demons of Egypt who hounded me. Together, we saved ourselves. And a child was born.

Later, I went to Greece and met and loved a wild boy, who spoke not. I healed him of his pain and horror, and trained him and educated him and faced those Greek Gods. Those same Greek Gods did I face, those who lived at the Omphallos at Delphi where I was conceived one night in passion and love, and in violation of those same Gods. We faced those Gods. And a child was born. A child, and a healing, too.

So I, Sybilla, became a mouthpiece for God, a sybil indeed, and a true "nymphomaniac," a bride, handmaiden, and lover of the Gods. It was then that I came to Paradise where I saw the Tree, met and heard Knight and Arab, Ronin and Julia, and told my tale.

MARIA, THE NUN

Mine is a story of how a woman of the present day, religious and Catholic, comes to terms with her God, her faith, and her most sinful self. I hardly dare to summarize my story, for I must then merely list such things as incest (with father, with brothers), heresy (a coming to know God as Mother), deceit and disruption. But I beg you not to misjudge me. The facts are true, but all is redeemed in my tale, for I found the great Teeter-Totter of God, the cross upon which can live the light and dark of me, the maiden and whore, as well as my brother and spirits. Because, from the very Center of that Teeter-Totter there emerged She who could combine all of these, the great Rose beyond the most virginal, she who is the once and future feminine of God. And my tale was told to all under the great Tree, upon which many crosses grew, including my own.

THE AFRICAN

I chose the title, "African", and it is indeed true of me, by right of inheritance from my forebears, and from my lived experience, even though I was born and lived in Detroit, U.S.A. Mine is a story of how I came to acquire that title, and what the consequences were, but I shall only hint at it here. Enough for me to say that I was a black man full of rage. After much pain and effort, to find something–I was not sure what. I sought roots, identity, history, and other such cliches. In truth, I sought a cure of my anger which was like a Kansas wind, an African wild fire, or... but my words were not enough. A long voyage through the length and breadth of Africa was not enough. Nor was reflection. But then...but then...In Ethiopia, I met my woman; in Abyssinia, I met my queen. Sheba, she was, and Sheba she seemed. She and I became alchemists of the soul. She and I baked and worked and transformed ourselves in the ancient art which began upon our continent and is still pursued on our continent. We found animal, and vegetable, and mineral and transformed them. We found body and mind and heart and changed them. And we found ourselves. We found and made the precious Stone, and joined in love. Rage was cured. And, when sailing upon the ship to return to Detroit, U.S.A., we came at night to another Paradise, where all the others came to tell their tales. And I told my own.

MAYA, THE YOGINI

I am Hindu, though born of an English father. Raised in the India of modern day I lived a full and rich life, more varied. I would imagine, than any westerner would guess. In middle life, however, I felt the need for a retreat, for an experience of the spirit which is typically sought by the men in our country, but less so by the women. I longed for a guru and wisdom, but could find none that I valued sufficiently. From a dream, and from desire, I resolved to go into the seclusion of the mountains and meditate, relying upon the help of the great Lord Shiva, Himself. So, I went, and I took with me mandalas and commentaries upon the great Kundalini Yoga. I took them and went off alone, leaving husband, children, lover—not irresponsibly, of course, since children were grown, husband had his own concerns, and lover was finding another.

I went and I practiced the Yoga of the Kundalini, all by myself, with only my supplications to the gods, with only my trust in Shiva and Shakti, with only my dreams and fantasies, and with only the pictures and commentary. Three years I remained. For three years, I meditated upon the centers, upon the Chakras, from Muladhara to Sahasrara, from anus to the top of the skull. I was alone and had many deep experiences, voyages in the soul and in space, in time and in dimensions one cannot speak about. Sexuality and hunger, passion and love, power and word, wisdom and vision: all these I faced. I confronted the transformations of God and Goddess, of Shiva and Shakti, as the Kundalini rose up my spine. And my story is a record of what I discovered. When I completed my work, I returned to Calcutta and my family, and was at peace. Suddenly, I was transported once again, but this time to the company of the seekers, the bank of Knight and Arab, Ronin and Julia, Sybilla and Maria, African and the rest. So, to them I told my tale, and there it is for those who wish to know of it.

THE OLD CHINESE MAN

Since each of my friends in this most esteemed company finds himself in a branch of religion or philosophy, albeit heretical, I suppose that I should also state my own. It is Taoistic, I might say, though I have a sone who is Christian, living far away, and my own education and experiences lead me to think of myself as a world-man. My tale, really, is a dialogue, between me and a book. Strange, you might think, for a man to speak with a book, but this is a very special one. It is called *I Ching*, our ancient and esteemed Book of Changes, which, indeed, is oracular and will respond to questions put to it. This text is no mere oracle, of course, but is a record of ancient wisdom and commentary from the Sages, including Confucius, himself. Now I, a man of the modern day, engaged this book, or the living "author" thereof, in conversation. I did not only put questions, but I spoke to the book directly, as if he were, indeed, an old man like myself. This extended conversation proved to be about myself and my arrogance, and about the book and its nature. And there were dreams and events, also. Much change took place, I think–in me, if not in the book. Yet, change took place in the cosmos, I think, in the family of the *I Ching*, in the family of my wife and children, and in the family of my soul. So, my tale is one of wisdom gained, by an Old Chinese Man.

THE MEDIUM

My name is Sophie-Sarah and my story is also with a book, though not entirely. Faced with the horror of the great Holocaust, and faced with my own mediumistic gifts, I resolved to take the dilemma of my people to the great text of Kabbala, itself, the Zohar, and to carry on a discussion with a Kabbalistic rabbi who came to me from Beyond. My tale is not a light one, and I do not believe that I can present a capsule of it which will either be clear enough to be valuable, or fair enough to the original. I can only hint that Hitler is to be found in the tale, and that the Names of God are there, and that mind and heart are challenged. The solution is my own, of course, and limited, but I am honored that the seekers have included me and that I found myself in their midst. I am awed to gaze upon the great Tree, which Kabbalists have always, always known. That tree grows with its roots in Heaven and reaches down into the world.

PSALMS

And, at last, there are poems, by each of the seekers. All try to express their experience, some in one poem, some in several. And these conclude *The Tree*, being the first volume, as it has been said, of a trilogy.

PART V
AN EAST-WEST TREE OF LIFE AND HYMNS

A chapter from
JUNGIAN PSYCHOLOGY AND THE PASSIONS OF THE SOUL
New Falcon Publications, First Edition, 1989

~ Seventh Center ~

Situation: Top of Head
Form: Diamond in Lotus
Color: Indigo
Gland: Pineal
Plexus: None
Animal: Lamb
Element: None
Function: Intuition (introverted-Jesus) and Feeling (introverted and extraverted-Mary)
Psychophysical quality: None
Organ of sense: None
Organ of action: None
Consciousness:

Jesus: the Christ. Man aware that he is a "son of God," a God-man, an incarnation of the spirit. Consciousness serves the every-unmanifested-ever-manifesting spirit above, while this self-same spirit ever-unfolds-ever-evolves-ever-manifests.

Hermes-Mercurius: Dark spirit of consciousness, which is the Holy Spirit, transforming and transformed. Man aware of his own dark side and his paradoxical nature.

Love: *Mary*: A God-woman. Love is compassionate, universal, forgiving. The soul is committed to poverty, chastity, obedience, to that self-same unincarnated spirit above; which is to say: receptive, open, attentive to it. The soul is wed to God, mother to God. The love is a union, producing ever-new consciousness and goes out to mankind, merciful.

Characteristic: Upper Trinity

(1) God-Father (unincarnated spirit) and God-Son (incarnated spirit) with the Holy Spirit (Hermes-Mercurius) as messenger and angel between God and man. (2) God-Father (spirit) wedded to Mary (soul), producing God-Son (consciousness). (3) Holy Spirit (messenger-angel) between God-Father (unincarnated spirit) and God-woman (Mary). A type of union producing intuition-consciousness and faith, love from God, and thence to mankind.

JESUS

Jesus, Jesus, Son of Man!
Consciousness are you? Knowing are you.
Then know, be aware! Tell me!
Tell me, in my humanity. Tell me.
How is it that God is a fire and a wind?
That God is a woman and a man?
That God is a circle and a square?
Tell me.

"I'll tell thee. I'll tell thee.
God is all one can see...
And not see.
What is not God?
Only that which is not blessed:
Out of sight of haloed light, holy fire;
Out of range of rugged wind, spirit's sire;
Not contained in human frame;
Not a form in geo'd game.
That is not God."

Then say, Sweet Jesus, say!
Say, man-light and man-wind!

Is irregular curve unblessed?
Is chaos not God?

"Yes and no.
For curve and chaos, unblessed,
Become God, blessed."

And man's task, Jesus?
Man's task?

"To give and receive:
Order and chaos
Curve and corruption
Form and be formed."

Blessing? Redemption."

God-man? "Man-God."

MARY

Mary poor, Mary real
Mary compassionate, Mary heal
Mary mother, Mary wife
Mary soul, Mary life

Open, Mary, open
Open belly heart and mind
To God-father, God-spouse, god-wind
Chase fire-tongues scaled you, transform you
Wild wind-hands caress you, possess you

Hermes dances on your soul
Angels cry, demons shriek

And God becomes a man.

God has crushed our human soul
Children cry, old ones shriek

Hell-blaze consumes us, torments us
Whirlwind embroils us, dements us

Close, Mary close
Close your robe and us entwine
From God-demon, God-villain, God-blind

Mary, my soul, my life
Mary, my mother, my wife
You are God-woman, heal
You bear God-men, real.

HERMES

Fly, great trickster, fly!
Fly to heaven, God's unseen eye
Fly to earth, man's unheard ear
Fly winged angel, fly near!

I know your darkness, Hermes, I know your light
I know your earthy jokes, your watery laugh
I know the fire of your alcheme bath

I will catch you in a vessel
In subtle body you will nestle
Moist-dry spirit flow through me
Solid-air ghost transform me

Foot, wing; man and God
Spirit, flesh; peas in pod
Top, bottom; you and me
Life, death; birds in tree

A pair, Binarius, I can see
A pair, Mercurius, you and me.
A third, most curious, rise from the sea
God-men created, for us to be.

LAMB

Lamb of God, what is it?
A weak, bleating thing? A sacrifice?
Yes, these.

But more:
Shorn of wool, vulnerable
Giving warmth, comfortable
Creature, created
Sensitive, soul-mated.

And more:
Hermes-Shepherd, Jesus-lamb
God is both, He said, "I AM"
Lamb of God is Son of God
Spirit of God is Shepherd
Hermes-Jesus, God and Man,
Gentle lamb and leopard!

And more:
The between. Mary.
And what is Mary?
The eye. You.
Soul as sheep, ewe. You.
Trinity: Shepherd, ewe, lamb
Such an animal! Such a God! Such a Man!

༺ Sixth Center ༻

Situation: Between eyebrows ("Third-eye")
Form: Eye in Diamond
Color: Violet
Gland: Pituitary
Plexus: None
Animal: Eagle (Zeus); Swan, Hawk, Crow, Raven, Wolf, Dolphin, Snake (all of Apollo); Owl (Athene); Cuckoo (Hera).
Element: None
Function: Thinking (introverted-Apollo, extraverted Athene) intuition (extraverted-Zeus, introverted-Hera)
Psychophysical quality: None
Organ of sense: None
Organ of action: None
Consciousness:

Zeus: All seeing, intuitive vision of the Many, the many possibilities for both consciousness and love. Is Father and, thus, leader (of Apollo and Athene); is also Son)to Kronos, the concrete): is born out of and overcomes the material state to finally unite with it; and Brother (to Poseidon and Hades), thus a democratic leader among equals. Lightning intuition, thundering emotion, visionary union. Producer of the creative.

Apollo: Thinking, reason, ordering, harmony. A son, a primarily a Brother, friend of man, but introverted, thus apart. Leader of the Muses (creativity), master of the python (prophecy), player of the lyre (controller of the seven centers). Reason, therefore, is the leader, moderator, and regulator of life, but is second to Zeus, the producer. Where Zeus is possibility, Apollo is structure and order.

Athene: Consciousness is for culture-building, civilization. Born of the mind, devoted to the creation of better worlds. The feminine realizing its individuality, consciously. The masculine serving the architecture of the more perfect society.

Hera: Consciousness of the single union, oneness. Solitary, solitude. When no union of consciousness, total darkness, negation of consciousness. Creative in spite of itself.

Love: Is Zeus-like (love of many), Apollo-like (love of structure and order, harmony), is Athene-like (love of realized culture), is Hera-like (impersonal to men, personal to God). Love is of consciousness, order, creativity, understanding.
Characteristic:
Upper quaternity
Paradox of the One (Hera, Athene) and the Many, (Zeus, Apollo). Mind.

ZEUS

Zeus, All-seeing, Lord of Many, Lord of one
Speak to me!
Tell of lightning-light and thunder-word
Tell of thee!

"In stone and stream I speak; in word and gleam.
I sound from high, the bell: but flow from low as well.
Does not the water whisper, just as thunder thrills?
Does not the rock shed light, just as lightning chills?"

A rock? Shed light?

"Yes, rocks shed light.
Look at dark mountain
When going down sun shines bright
In narrow valley's slant
On glacier's snowy coldness. Look.
Does not the rock reflect the light?
When tree is dark?"

It does.

"Then think. Think."

I'll think. I'll think.
Nature shows the light of God. Even the rocks do it.
Nature's stone—the self—speechless, changeless, hard…

Shows the light of God.
Look at rocks, unchanging. See God.
Look at stream of life, changing. See God.

I see, oh Zeus, I see.
Zeus is Lord of Rocks, Lord of Streams.
For there, in rocks and streams, He speaks
As well as lightning fire and thunder sound.
In earth and water, fire and air, He speaks.
And I shall listen.

And see, my Lord, and see.
For does not the light shine bright in narrow valley's darkness?
Does not the ray persist as cold wind shivers skin?
Does not the Lord return the joy when deep depression's past?
And make me laugh with warm sun's blaze, creation's eye, at last?

APOLLO

Lord Apollo! A hymn to you!
A hymn.
I see you, Lord
I see.

Dark curls, muscled flesh: Greek God.
Handsome face, open look: potent man.
Sleek snake in left hand, shaped lyre in right
Aura's gold about your head.
I see you, Lord.
I see.

But speak to me, Lord, speak!
Speak of creation, Muses
Of prophecy, snake
Of wisdom, light.

"All in the snake, all.
From snake to lyre to light.
I pray, you pray.
Hold.

"Would you create, serve Muse?
Then listen, hold.
Would you predict, be wise?
Then listen, hold.

"Hold and listen, then sing.
And singing, think.
And thinking, pray.
And praying, feel.
And feeling, know.
This the wisdom, this the light."

I hold, Lord, I hold.
The snake coils in my belly and rises, rises.
She rises, I hold.
And holding, know.

Python's flame breathes air to sacred lyre
Muse's strings sound mood to golden fire
Apollo's sun, Halo's glow.

"Never let go. Never let go."

HERA

Hera, Dark Goddess, Witch of the Eye,
I salute you!
Hail, fierce Goddess, jealous of the God,
I fear you.

I kneel to your aloneness, solitary
I bow to your withdrawal, darkness
I bow, I kneel, I fear, salute
But I weep.

No love, Goddess? No care?
Only jealousy, demands?
Only pain, no thought of Man?
Only You?

"Only me...
And you...
And God.
Only."

Bind my tongue...stillness
Cover my eyes...darkness
Love my Lord...fierceness
Like you.

Alone, Hera-sola
One, hera-mona
Devoted, fierce
Whole or null.

I bow, Goddess,
I know, Goddess,
I love, Goddess.
Like you.

ATHENE

Athene, fierce maid, city's wisdom, speak to me!
Tell of building's beauty, civic joy
Weave the dreams of pattern, thoughts of order
Show the Hero's way.

"The way is winding, you know.
The light is slanting, you know.
From winding build the straight
From slanting form the round.
Circle and square, you know.
The Eye, you know."

If I know, Goddess,
Why do I ask?
If I know, Goddess,
Why implore?
"You know man, you know.
To speak, inform,
To mold, be 'informed,'

You know."

We know, Goddess, we know.
Born of the God, we.
Born of the head, we.

A thought, 'in-formed'
God thinks man, and man thinks God,
In-formed.
Man makes the world, the world makes man,
Re-formed.

Help us think, Maiden, help us when you can
Help us know the form, help us shape the plan.
Show us the straight, bare the winding
Reveal the slant, showing the binding.

EAGLE

Eagle-bird, lofty!
Soul of Zeus, crafty!
So proud you are, aloof
Winged hateur, beaked tooth.
I see your height, your matchless vision
I know your might, your intuition
Spirit soars, nests on mountain
Thunder roars, heaven's fountain
Eagle-bird, far seer!
Soul of God, man's leader!

ANIMALS OF APOLLO

Apollo! Moderator! Leader of Muses! Player of Seven-Stringed Lyre!
Seven Centers lead You! Seven animals, too! Separate, together, entire!
Snake: galling Goddess, time transformer, love of life
Dolphin: want of waters, hungry hoarder, wishes' wife
Wolf: mighty mover, fiery fighter, passioned power

Raven: heart of hunger, spirit seeker, torment's tower
Crow: calling crier, speaking sagely, telling tales
Hawk: sharp-eyed seer, clear-eyed creature, vanquishing veils
Swan: land, air and water; bird-fish transformer,
God-man-transcender, triad uniter.

CUCKOO

Cuckoo. Hera's bird.
Sings in Spring,
Time when Marriage Mistress is at peace,
    with her Lord.
  no jealousy, no rages
  no tantrums, no cages.
Cuckoo. Bird of Goddess.
Faithful Singer.
Time when she's no more in solitude,
    in blessed union
  no pain, no resentment
  full reign, full contentment.

OWL

Owl. Oo Oo Oo
All know your voice. Your eyes.
    Athene's bird, wise.
But do they know your wit?
    Your song is but a laugh?
    Your wisdom is but half?
Inner smile, by moon is lit.

Owl. Oo Oo Oo
All know your voice. Your eyes.
    Athene's bird, wise.
But do they know your passion?
    For beauty's form, a glowing face?
    For culture's norm, a golden grace?
Aesthetic maid, intense inaction!

☞ Fifth Center ☜

Situation: Throat
Form: Circle; Wheel with nine spokes
Color: Blue-gray
Gland: Thyroid
Plexus: Pharyngeal
Animal: Turtle, Dove (Aphrodite Urania); Winged Horse, Pegasus (Muses)
Element: Ether
Function: Expression and Communication
Psychophysical quality: "Akashic": space-giving
Organ of sense: Hearing
Organ of action: Mouth
Consciousness:

A power God of the passions dwells here; a dark spirit who tests and tries the soul–like Bluebeard–and pushes all the creative products of the soul back into itself–like Ouranos. The type of consciousness is fierce and artistic, in which creation is compelled to express itself in a spiritual way. Central is expression and communication, in which man realizes himself as a God-man in terms of his creative work. The paradigm is Hephaistos, the creator. The drama of life is expressed as art and creation; man knows that God dreams life creatively and so–at this level–does man.

Love:

The Muses, representing the multiplicity of the soul's creative gifts of expression. This expression comes into being from the union of the One great dark spirit with the Many of the soul's creative potentialities. Love is in the form of Aphrodite Urania, a great spiritual love which is a oneness from which all the maniness of the Muses emerge and to which they return. Love is a creative passion and a passion for creation.

Characteristic:

    Upper Unity
        Dynamic (One spirit, many potentials)
        Creativity
    Speak dark spirit, speak Heavenly Father,
        speak Ouranos, express!

Speak brutal lover, speak Devilish Brother,
    speak Bluebeard, confess!
Speak to such a one as I!

Conniving creature, crippled, cuckold, like Hephaistos am I.
Lacerated lover, limited, lupold, like Hera's son am I.
Speak to such a one as I!

"I speak; I speak:
Heavy, heavy, do I lean
From Heaven's height to earth's sore spleen.
Each night I come and sleep, weep.
Each night create, fecundate.
Each day I turn away
From Gaia's heart to sky-light's sheen.

Have you known such pain, such sorrow?
Have you known this strain, dread of morrow?
Daily change, endless round of God.
"Create, create' she says; 'An end, an end,' say I.
'I grown, I groan!' says she; 'No more new,' I cry.
Thus brutal, rough am I, not mild
Thus my glee at smothered child.

But son deposed me from my power
Do not fret it, do not glower
Castrate God does love create
Muse's soul takes shape from weight.
Heaven's earth travails no more
Creatured art is man at core.
Love fulfills the earth's creation
In spirit's growth, emancipation.

Dream on the tale, evolve the myth
Weave the light in bones and pith.
The web's dark tangle is the ground
With rain-drop jewels of speech, the sound.
Creative light heals endless round
Let word and joy and life abound!
The 'endless round' is God's own form, at last
And man's blind state of circled grief is past."

KLEIO

Kleio, Giver of Fame, Enfolder of History
Sing to me, embrace me!

"I embrace Hephaistos, serve God
But tongue-tied poet, mere sod?
No history, no fame, Naught inspire, nothing claim."

You speak, oh Muse, all the same
You come when called your name
You respond when I implore
You never close the door.

Doors ajar shed some light
Little men claim some sight
Mortal mean spark God
Creatures come from sod.

"I smile, 'tis true
I'll smile, for you."

OURANIA

Ourania, Heavenly Muse, star-gazer
Sing to me, embrace me!

"I embrace all men, need no song
Stars abound, sing sphere's music
Speak Fate.

Not Nemesis, nor Aidos, but Time
And Psyche's form stretched taut
Show pattern, show web."

I know Muse, I know.
At night, as I gaze
In quiet, as I muse
I know.

Patterned Fate.
Destiny from Character, they say
And they are right.
But character is chosen, is it not?
In Ourania's realm?
Before the birth?
Karma's choice?

"'Tis true. 'Tis true."

MELPOMENE

Melpomene, Singer, Tragedy's face
Sing to me, embrace me!

"Would be enclosed by me?
Not likely.
Would you sing my song?"

Your song I'd sing, your clutch evade
Who seeks pain's claw, illusion's shade?
Not I.

"It comes all the same."
It comes.
"And, coming sometimes teaches."
"Sometimes not.
Sometimes not."

Dark face, sad face.
Always there.
"Always there."

Accept? Transform?
"Try."

Why?
"Sigh."

THALEIA

Thaleia, Comic Muse, Festive One, are you there?
Sing to me, embrace me!

"Comic song is easy:
Laugh at self.
Easy, but hardest.
Who can do it?"
Too much pain, too much conceit.

"But that's the one who laughs, man
He who knows
Too much pain and vanity.
In knowing, laughing;
To him, I sing.

TERPSICHORE

Terpsichore, You Who Enjoy Dancing, Mistress of the Lyre,
Sing to me, embrace me!

"No word, man, move!
Move to heart's desire.
Move to the dance,
Move to the lyre!

God's word is a line
Snake flet on the spine.
Move!"

KALLIOPE

Kalliope, Of the Beautiful Voice, Muse of Heroic Song,
Sing to me, embrace me!

"Hero's song is a sad tune
Have you known it?
To labor mightily, Heracles
To seek endlessly, Odysseus
Wander confusedly, Perseus

Suffer painfully, Prometheus
That's the Hero's song.

And for what to labor and wander?
For what to seek and suffer?
For fame? For art? For love? For mankind?
None of these."

Not even for God?

"Not even for God."

For the song.
For the singing.
Even in silence.
Even when none can hear.
Thus does the true hero sing.

"And thus is his voice made mellow by my own.
Heroe's song: Kalliope. For itself."

ERATO

Erato, Awakener of Desire, Muse of the Dance
Sing to me, embrace me!

No word from you, like Terpsichore,
But I see you, feel you.

Dark passion rising from within, awakened.
Limbs curl, flesh fulls, sex stirs
The flow.
Life awakened, the body moves to God's music.
Who can listen to the sound?
Who can flow and form?

Not I, Muse, not I!
Yes I, Muse, Yes I.
I can, can not; will, will not.
In this, embraced, in this, awakened.

For thus, the Dance.

EUTERPE

Euterpe, Giver of Joy, Flute Muse,
Sing to me, embrace me!

"I do not sing, I play!
In playing, joy!"

Play: How can a grown man play?
Tell me, pray.

"In playing, a flute.
In playing, an act.
In playing, a love.

"Thus making music, feeling
Thus making drama, being
Thus making love, living."

Thus Joy, Muse Mistress,
Thus Joy, Euterpe!

""Thus Joy."

POLYMNIA

Polymnia, Of Many Hymns, Muse of Story-Telling
Sing to me, embrace me!

"That I have done, and that I do.
And that you know already.
No poet you, nor your fathers, too,
But teller of tales, heady."

Like you, Muse, like you.
Do I speak, Muse, or is it you?
"No matter, we speak.
In speaking, knowing
In knowing, serving

"Story-teller of God, Him.
Muse of God, hymn
Fool of God, hmm."

APHRODITE

Aphrodite, Mistress of Muses
Sing to me, embrace me!

"You, Man, sing to me.
You, Man, embrace me!"

I will, Goddess, I will.
You it is I love, adore.
You will I serve, evermore.

As nine-faced Muse
In action and strife
In word and in image
As love in my life.

TURTLE AND DOVE OF APHRODITE URANIA

All see the turtle and the dove!
All glimpse the animals of love!
The one: to sing in spring, renewal bring.
The other: join together, pair forever.

Yet turtle, alone: two shells, slow. Speaks not at all.
   Yet speaks, alone: in time's flow. At God's call.
And dove, together: white song, coo. Sings long, sings new.
   Yet silent, when alone: lonely view. Sorrow's strong, full of rue.

So, the soul, in love's expression, God's discretion.
Silent, pain. Flowing, rain.
Turtle crawls and slowly speaks: stammer, stutter
Dove flies high and spirit seeks: clamor, flutter.

Turtle shells are two, in one
Dove's love union, same.
One and many, rays of sun
Love's expression, name.

Name? Aphrodite, Urania love!
Fame! Soul united, turtle-dove!

PEGASUS

Pegasus, winged horse, mighty mare of Muses!
Pegasus, fearful force, in you flesh-spirit fuses.

Medusa's blood, the witch defeated, flows in you
Poseidon's sod, earthquake trod, horse fleshes you

Yet wings have you, the mark
Soul's flight have you, the spark.
Blood and earth, transformed
Creation's task, performed.

A flight, of ages
A soar, of sages
The spirit's task in stages
A poet's passion rages

Pegasus, spirit's steed
Muses' heart, spirit's need
Pegasus, spirit's seed
Flesh made word, spirit's deed!

⌒ Fourth Center ⌒

Situation: Heart
Form: Star of David, Seal of Solomon
Color: Orange
Gland: Thymus
Plexus: None
Animal: Lion (Jacob), Gazelle (Ruth), Cow (Demeter).
Element: Air
Function: Feeling (Extraverted-Demeter and Ruth; Introverted-Jacob)
Psychophysical quality: Movement
Organ of sense: Touch, feel
Organ of action: Penis
Consciousness:

Jacob. Struggling with God, serving God with passion and sense of chosenness, becoming Israel. Personal in relation to the transpersonal. Consciousness is intense, and the vision is fierce and commanding. The impersonal becomes personal, individual.

Love:

Demeter, or another form of *Aphrodite* Urania, maternal, but outflowing to men in the world, personal. Is also Ruth, love as devoted, accepting. Love is expressed in *relationship* and not as a universal and primarily transpersonal love as in the type of Mary. Love is in time and place. Like the God of the Hebrews, the divine is realized in history, in time, in the human condition on earth. Feeling is intense and focused on values, the worth of man in the sight of God.

Characteristic: Upper Duality.

(Relationship is central: Man to god and men with each other.

JACOB

Jacob, Jacob, wrestler with God
As brother and heir, I call you!
Wounded, strong, thigh-marked, proud
Like Zeus himself, I see you!

"No foreign Gods will I know!
Nor kneel before stone pagan Baal!
To only the Lord do I bow,
For each of the others, gall!"

Jacob, Jacob, with angel blessedness,
Chosen son of the Lord!
Is not Elohim a Maniness?
Is Esau just part of the horde?

God speaks to men in many tongues
Not alone in Hebrew, nor only to the Jew.
In Sanskrit, Greek, his voice is sung
He chooses mankind, too.

" 'T true, my heir, 'tis true.

"Struggler with God is server of God
Whether chosen or not, you're His son.
The many-faced Lord given men but one nod
The many names are but One.

"Unspoken, unknown, He chooses us all
No escape from His eye or His heart
Whether chosen or choosing, Mankind must stand tall
For God's love is the way and the art.

"With wrestle or wrath, we flow to the Lord
To men we pour out our passion,
Flame's feeling like leaves, chest's castle our sword
Heart's justice for all is our Reason."

Jacob, Jacob, your chest on my own
Our hearts, in unison, chosen
Our thigh-wounds, too, from angel-tear sewn
Our strength in our feelings, risen.

DEMETER, RUTH, APHRODITE
SISTERS OF THE HEART

Demeter, Sorrowing Mother: Keep faith
Ruth, Devoted Sister: Hold fast
Aphrodite, Passioned Lover: Flow out

All names are but one name: All loves are but one
Caring, loyal, passioned: Mother, Maiden, Mistress
Goddess One or Goddess Three: Flowing Love of the heart

Will you speak, Goddess, Dweller in the Heart?

"I will speak. I will speak"

Speak soft, words of love, speak low
The murmuring heart sounds a gentle beat
The passionate flame not a blaze
The fire of love sheds a delicate glow
The rhythm not measured in days.

The love of the heart is a loyal devotion
Commitment and caring its names
The love of the heart rises deep from the ocean
Connection and warmth are its aims.

Gentle leaves, warm delicate pulse
Are not heart's only mark
Love's personal, passionate, profound
The love of the heart is no lark.
Gentle and glowing: power and passionate
Goddess: Personal

Relationship

LION

King proud
Roaring loud
Chest-breath chosen,
Passionate.
Bellows air flows in

Heart's word flows out
Who can dare ration it?
The Lord, of course, the lion's master
Chooses and forms, commanding
Lion power, tamed by God
Jacob power, lamed by God
To serve and be served, demanding
Lion love, love of Lord
For this does heart beat faster

GAZELLE

Gentle gazelle
Airy antelope
Delicate deer

Your name is Ruth, graceful
Your name is Ruth, admirable
Your name is Ruth, devotional

Ruth love: loyal to tell
Ruth love: royal gazelle

COW

Careful cow, caring
Chewing cud, reflecting
Nurturing cud, nestling

Demeter, searchingly serving
Demeter, devotedly living
Demeter, generously giving

Demeter love: mother milk
Cow-eyed One: soft as silk

⌒ Mid-Point ⌒

Situation: Between heart and solar plexus
Form: Tree with Man
Color: Yellow
Gland: None
Plexus: None
Animal: Not animal, but plant, the tree.
Element: None
Function: Meditation (intuition and sensation)
Psychophysical quality: None
Organ of sense: None
Organ of action: None
Consciousness:

Meditative. A place of *Buddha*, under the Bo Tree. Man in his full humanness and connection with nature. An ego center in relation to Self. Detachment from possession by "demons" (lower centers) and "inflation" (upper center), Man and woman exist humanly between spirit (center above) and matters (centers below). Consciousness is "awareness"; there is sensitivity and involvement in life, but separation also. Enlightenment. No-mind.

Love:

Self-love is the seed of the tree of all-embracing love. The greater Self is the expression of the oneness of all things. Buddha is the realization of four kinds of love-compassion (as below), and is at work all the time.

Meta: All embracing love; oneness of life (people, animals, plants)

Karuna: Compassion, pity, pain in another's pain.

Mudita: Sympathetic joy, pleasure in another's pleasure, friendliness.

Upeksha: Impartiality, objective state, understanding of the fact that everything in its origin is conditional.

Characteristic: Lower Dynamic Unity
   Lower Dynamic Unity
   Enlightenment through meditation; detachment, stillness.

BUDDHA

Meditating man
Silent, empty, nature, whole
Fishing with no pole

Compassionate man
Smiling, sharing, showing, stand
Feeling with no hand

***

Meta-love oneness
Life teeming, embracing can
Buddha tree, fly, man

Karuna-love care
Compassion, pity, suffer
Buddha man Mother

***

Detaching woman
Separate, stable, seeing flaw
Caring with no claw

Enlightened woman
Lamplight, lovelight, lifelight, laugh
Wholing with no half

***

Upeksha-love know
To see, detach, enlighten
Buddha egg, hatch hen

Mudita-love joy
Laughter is enlightenment
Buddha friendly lent

TREE

Reflect, please, on trees
A tree is an animal
Which moves not at all

~ Third Center ~

Situation: Diaphragm
Form: Triangle with dot
Color: Red
Gland: Adrenal
Plexus: Solar
Animal: Goat (Dionysos), Cock (Persephone)
Element: Fire
Function: Emotion
Psychophysical quality: Expansion, heat
Organ of sense: Sight and color
Organ of action: Anus
Consciousness:

Knowing sacrifices itself to Being, Emotion is more important than knowing; Being is more important than becoming. A "now" of movement. *Dionyso*s: the center where union becomes disunion, where that which is old dies, where heat of passion transforms desire from below; leading up to the no-mind center above it. Consciousness is awareness through emotion: *Dionysos*. But there is also the experience of conflict, strife, power. Consciousness is awareness through conflict of opposites: Ares.

Love:

Love is of the many experiences, many emotions. Love is ecstatic, abandonment. *Persephone*.

Characteristic: Lower Trinity

Transformation through movement, e-motion.
Power.

ARES

Ares, Lord of Strife
Speak to me, inform me!

"Life is conflict, battle
Fight with me, wage war
Know the struggle's core

"Swarm in rage, serve God
Contain the heat, grow strong
Power's use, our song.

"A man fights well who serves a cause
Battle's cry is tempered
The soul's a field of war which gnaws
With conflict's pain it's embered.

"A man's transformed by Ares strife
Aggression's sting is softened
Who holds the struggle, reveres the life
For God, his soul is strengthened.

"Serve the Lord, take Strife
Accept the conflict of soul
How else can a man serve God in his life?
How else bring the parts to a whole?"

DIONYSOS

Dionysos, Lord of Passion,
Speak to me, inform me!

"Life is emotion, passion
Come with me, be wild
Know abandon's child.

"Drink sea-wine, taste God
Shed the forms, grow free
Passion's pull, our plea.

"A man's alive who feels intense
Dry meaning's words are whetted
The soul's a sea of passion which rends
All change in emotion embedded.

"A man's transformed in passion's season
Dionysos wine dismembers
Who suffers a madness regains his reason
When for God, his soul remembers

"Serve the Lord, take emotion
Accept the passion of soul
How else can a man find change, transformation?
How else sense that God is a whole?"

PERSEPHONE

Persephone, Ecstatic One, Inward One!
Come out of Hades, come out of the depths!
Rejoin us in the world of your Mother, Demeter.
Rejoin us in the place where words can be heard,
And tell us of the Love in a central place,
Tell us of the Dionysiac place of ecstasy.
Tell us of the realm between Hell and Heaven, between
    Hades and Hearts.
Tell us!

"You tell me.
Sing to me your hymn.
Sing and I shall reply."

Persephone, Goddess, we have known the love ecstatic.
We have felt the orgastic explosions of passion,
    kept up and nourished.

We have the daylong love, the nightlong love.
We have known the pocket-kept desires, passions both held
    and let go.
We have known control and abandon, surrender and battle,
    until at last
We have thrown ourselves into Your hands.

"Not my hands, man, but those of Lord Dionysos, Lord Hades,
    Lord Poseidon.
Not my hands, man.
Mine is a dark deep ecstasy of innerness, and aloneness.
Mine is raped by another.

"Mine is an aloneness of a flower, a purple.
Mine is an ecstasy out of mind, out of heart, out of all but self.
Mine is not a Hera solitude, turning away in pain.
Mine is a Persephone solitude, turning away in pleasure,
intensity.

"The soul adores itself, devours itself.
The soul takes in itself alone.

"And then, and then...
Should two souls thus devour themselves, be alone,
  in solitude,
Then can they meet in that bridge of flow, of passion,
  ecstasy shared."

Thus, Goddess, you are she who can live in Hades, in Belly,
  and in Heart.

Thus, Goddess, you are she who can bridge the realms!

"Most at home alone, man, most at home alone.
At the place where passion dwells.
Passion, ecstatis, Alone."

A mystery, the mystery of self, out of self.

COCK

Strutting cock, bird of power world
Why so proud, a fowl who cannot fly?
You do not fly, but die each night and go to the Underworld
Each day you're born and crow the dawn when morning sun
  you spy.

You call and claim that death's not true
That there's a resurrection
Persephone bird, proud day for you
Rebirth, the Two's connection.

GOAT

Goat-God, wild, you stubborn power!
Who can stay you, not just cower?
And why should goat be goaty power?
Stubborn, strong, semen sour?

Does not the goat bleat?
Is not his flesh meat?
Does he not suffer heat?
Are hooves not also feet?
Dionysos God, this animal
Scape-goat, victim, killable
Sacrifice, torn apart, dissolved anew in carnival
Sacred vice, short at start, and born anew, not stillable.

Goat, goaty, fine
Powered, weak, sublime
The Now, in passing time
God's goat is in His sign.

⁀ Second Center ⁀

Situation: Belly
Form: Crescent
Color: Green
Gland: Lyden
Plexus: Hypogastric
Animal: Horse, Bull, Fish (Poseidon) Sparrow, Ram, Hare (Aphrodite Pandemos)
Element: Water
Function: Sensation (introverted and extraverted)
Psychophysical quality: Contraction
Organ of sense: Taste
Organ of action: Hand
Consciousness:

Desire and its opposite, negation of desire; hunger to take in, consume. To know is to devour. Experience of difference between self and others. *Poseidon* with the trident: the thunder of desire moving in sea (unconscious), on land (in consciousness), brings activity and change into life. Consciousness is awareness of lack, of want.

Love:

Love in space, in the flesh. Sex as transformer of energies experienced in sensations. Sensation is central. is love as *Hestia*: the hearth and nest needs. Is love as *Baubo*: the belly moving, dancing and laughing in its own sensations and hunger. Is love as *Aphrodite Pandemos*: love in the world, love concrete, sex in all its forms as desire and union in the flesh.

Characteristic: Lower Trinity

Hunger: search for inclusion, extension, expansion
Need and Desire.

HESTIA, BAUBO, APHRODITE

Hestia! Hearth!
Warm nest, cosy fire.
Baubo! belly!
Hungry maw, hot desire.

What powers through your blood!
What claims!
What channels in your flood?
What tames?

Nor are two of you enough,
It seems.
Aphrodite speaks, love rough,
in dreams.

In Belly place, Pandemos
The human race, you claim us.
What trinity! what power!
What energy! Life's tower!

Nest and hunger, sensuality.
Are these your love? Reality?
Hard to perceive, without grief.
Hard to conceive, compel belief.

For your passions overwhelm me, possess me.
Your drives overcome me, transgress me.
All limits–foreign to your eyes.
Restraint–illusion in the skies.

Can love a belly labyrinth be?
Can want, desire, be the key?
Buddha thought so, Jesus, too.
The one overcame, the other, too.

But you are females, Goddesses!
No male corset ties, no bodices!...
Save when you wish...
Save when you wish...

You bow to no male
To man or God, not for sale.
Save when you wish...
Save when you wish.

For Desire's your name
And it will have claim
From Goddess and man
From woman and Pan.

Together we'll worship
In cave's labyrinth, adore.
Our vessel, a hearth ship
Our course, toward the "more."

Inclusion, our aim
Sensation, our game
Life in the flesh, replete
Love in the world, concrete.

Hestia! dancing!
Baubo! prancing…
'D'Dite! romancing.
Man! enhancing.

POSEIDON

Mighty Poseidon, fierce God, thunderer!
Horse-maker, water king, plunderer!
You move our selves to hunger and to know.
Your trident stings and life begins to flow.

Awareness?
Desire!
Activity?
Aspire!

To love is to consume
To rest is but a tomb
To know is to devour
Each instant like an hour.

Take in, take in,
Unite!
Extend, advance,
More light!

But Pegasus, you fly
Restless quest soars high.
Poet-horse stamps fountain
Seas depths produce the mountain.

So, God, you give and take
Desire and negate
Life's flow is yours to start
You appear and then depart.

Your realm is land-sea stronghold
Your mystery is threefold
With brothers Zeus and Hades
With Goddesses, three ladies.

They are three, and you are three
Restless, moving, changing
Swimming deep, shaking free
Our stable earth endangering.

Wise men fight and then submit
Knowing belly madness
Hero's quest is roasting spit
Labyrinth's realm a sadness

But I can know, fell your staff
Sense the pull of power
There is joy in Nature's laugh
Even Buddha held the flower.

Sense, want, hunger, know
All these convey your meaning
Trident's sting is made to glow
When there are mixed with feeling.

Bellied heart? How?
Heartened belly!
Wanting light? Now!
Lighting want, not sully.

Desert's darkness opens clear
To green oasis, standing near
Water-desire, Poseidon-wet
Trident-love, Poseidon-net

You, God, will have your way
Who, my Lord, will say you nay?
With Goddesses-three and grace and bloom
Three and One, magnificent plume!

Mighty Poseidon, fierce God, thunderer,
Horse-maker, water King, plunderer
You move our selves to hunger and to know
Your trident stings and life begins to flow.

SPARROW, RAM, AND HARE
OF APHRODITE PANDEMOS

Sensual sparrow, rutting ram, hare in heat!
Lascivious creatures of Aphrodite!
    Sparrow shrieking
    Ram reeking
    Hare hunting

Do you covet and lust?
Or can you love and take care?
Is instinct just a force and a must?
Or can instinct show love and be fair?
    All yearning, squabbling, taking
    All burning, gabbling, mating.
Does Goddess speak Pandemos?
Is yours the love that claims us?

Such is love and lust for union
Such is love in belly life
Such is love in deep communion
Even love for man and wife!

Without the belly love there are no children
Without the belly love there is no growth
Sparrow songs to nature hearken

Goddess speaks to us in both

Is ram not father of the lamb?
And sparrow sister to the dove?
The hare's no hurt to beast or man
All three belong to Goddess Love!

HORSE, BULL, FISH
ANIMALS OF POSEIDON

Poseidon's horse is earthquake formed

He stamped and horse resulted
The God's demand, the earth transformed
His want, in life exulted

Is bull no less than sacred horse?
Is he not conucopia?
Taurus sign is vital force
Taurine time, Utopia.

And fish, the dolphin, West's "makara"
Swims the depths and knows
Of life's creation, strife, "samara"
Laughs at pretense, pose

All three, the fish, the bull, the horse
Are tynes in sacred fork
Poseidon rides his three-fold course
His trident tries all talk

Until the horse has Pegasus wings
Until the bull is transformed
Until the fish in dolphin-speech sings
Until nature in words is informed

But trident's dynamic, man's life and his being
Depend on their animals three
The flow of their presence in body and feeling
Is to sense vital joy and be free!

⌒ First Center ⌒

Situation: Anus (Between anus and genitals)
Form: Square
Color: Brown
Gland: Gonads
Plexus: Perineum
Animal: Dog and Cat
Element: Earth
Function: Sensation as Reality (seen and not-seen)
Psychophysical quality: Cohesion
Organ of sense: Smell
Organ of action: Feet
Consciousness:

Kronos: Consciousness is concrete, everyday life, the structure of society, family, etc. as "given." Limitation of space and time. Awareness of matter, limits. Reality as the concrete.

Hades: At a deeper level is Hades, the Magician; Lord of transformation; changing, and shaping itself ever anew in images in the spiritual sense, but with concrete effect. Reality as evanescent.

Love:

Rhea: Daughter of Earth and Sky, wife of Kronos, she is the Great Mother. Her love is of the "given," in family, society, structure. She is mother of all changes and futures) of the Gods), though content with what "is."

Hecate: At a deeper level is Hecate, the Witch, Mistress of Magic. Her effect is indirect, she is mover of occult forces. As such, there are dark changes, there is a material web of relationships and love, but it is "below," is not apparent like Aphrodite's web, it is unseen. Love of Magic, of effecting changes in matter indirectly; and Magic of Love, of coming together in occult, non-rational ways.

Characteristic: Lower Quaternity
    Concretization; Transformation, Indirect Effect

KRONOS

Kronos, God of Structure, Lord of Time!
Kronos, God of "Givens," most sublime
You who scythed the heaven, bled the sky
You who make the leaven, tell me why!

Speak to me of limits, tell of stricture
Speak to me of matter, show a picture.
Are you narrow, cruel, or calm?
Are you small, or nature's balm?

"Form is given, that you know
Hard to transcend, hard to let go.
It is not only I who worship forms,
Man builds square houses, fearing storms.

"Did I not cut oppression? 'Make' love?
Am I for possession, freedom shove?
Paradise is my aim and was my father's claim.
Hold what is, say I, until the stars draw night.

"My son and I, we make a pair
In Isles of Blest, we find our lair.
Possibility is endless, reality contains
Ambition's soar is boundless, modesty restrains.

"You need us both to live, you know
None succeed so let us go.
Reality's a God, do accept it.
Touch the sod, don't reject it.

"Draw it over like a blanket, feel no rupture
Taste the peace of order, sense the structure
There's your picture, most sublime
Reality's a blanket, not a crime!"

Kronos, God of Structure, Lord of Time
Kronos, God of "givens," most sublime
Tell me how, in your dominion
Structure's clamp is not a pinion?

"Narrowness is in mind's eye found
When it feels frustration
Peace of limits, freely bound
Brings cruel pain's cessation.

Let limits be lived, yea, limits be loved!
For 'possibilities' fulfillment.
The hand of potential in Reality is gloved
The union of both in the moment!"

HADES

Hades, Hades, Magician!
Lord of Transformation!
Speak to me.

"Change, change, change, no words
Image, moving matter
Change in Hades realm, dark birds
Then fly, they make no clatter

"Ionic dot, atomic spot
Movement, transformation
Historic rot, artistic plot
All change, imagination

"All that is, is all that was
Motion myth, mutation
Sacred thought is fertile fuzz
New gods, the soul's elation

"What is time but earth's rotation?
What is space but measure?
Permanence is permutation
Numbers form a treasure.

"Circle to dot, dot to space
Space to square and repeat
This is the story of the human race
This is the magical feat.

"But do not despair of the changes
No fault, no reproach and no blame
Soul's growth through the cosmos ranges
God's means and God's ends are the same.

"Change is true, but do not brood
The bread of life is 'illusion'
Fantasy is psyche food
The blood of life's transfusion.

"So come with me to my true place
And glimpse the magic station
'Transform' say I, at dizzy pace
Rebirth, soul's destination.

And glimpse the magic station
"Transform' say I, at dizzy pace
Rebirth, soul's destination.

"My realm, 'as far beneath the earth', they say,
'As earth beneath the sky.'
Which is to say, another way,
I am, indeed, nearby.

"So play with me, change with me
Follow soul's transformation
And register, see, all the flow greet with glee
Fear no dark consternation.

"Dark sun sheds its light
Hell's moon casts no veil, nor derision
To feel its full might, one must see its full sight
Should one wish to partake of its vision.

"Divination's the key, awareness of me
The clue to magic's reality.
Soul's state not a fee, soul's death not to be
Mind's mold is spirituality."

RHEA

Rhea, Great Mother, Daughter of Earth, Daughter of Sky
Rhea, Wife of Kronos, Mother of Giants, will You draw nigh?
Tell how love is "given" and contains
Tell how love is present and can change.

"Pain I know, to pain respond.
Baby's cry, man's despond.
For birth is my lot, to bear and rebear
Child's loss is love's clot, earth's failure, despair.

"I feel all pains and sorrows
I know all future morrows
Yet knowing and being
Makes no change in feeling

"My husband and I love that which 'is'
Life's flow is mine, square's order is his.
My Kronos and I love all the 'given'
Yet change is my nature, toward change am I driven.

"Through permanence is mine, I am earth and the sea
Evolution and future flow out from me
To be and behold is man's lot in the world
To see and take hold, not falter, be whirled

"Zeus and Kronos, Father and Son
Potential and Actual, struggle's done
Union of change and permanence
Wisdom of sky, earth's residence

"A state, a time, a moment known
Permanent creation, earth's wind blown
Moment felt, instant tasted,
Paradise on earth, nothing wasted.

"Do you see? Can you rise?
Come with me to Paradise?
Do you feel? Can you tell?
Paradise is next to Hell!"

HECATE

Hecate, Hecate, Mistress of the Magic
Hecate, Hecate, Goddess of the Tragic
How much I have suffered you, hated you!
How much I have ruffled you, slayed you!

Though I would not be thwarted by you, ruled by you
I cannot be parted from you, fooled by you
So speak, Great Goddess, speak and tell!
Speak to me the sounds from Hell!

"Sounds words, space flight
Two things joining matter's plight.
Between the poles, magnetic measure
Indirect, effect I treasure.

"Broom and cat, my ornament
Sweep and Eye, my nightly bent
Do I see clearly, darkly?
Do I fight fiercely, smartly?

"Effect I would produce, magic
Reason to seduce, tragic
Hades realm, light and dark
Hecate realm, spite and spark."

Goddess, spider, weaver of webs!
Hecate, Rider, leader
I fear you, I hate you
I love you, create you!

Hecate, spider, weaver of webs!
No shield from you have I
From bare projections, I fair die!

Vulnerable am I, bleeding
Creature am I, needing
Paralysis from you, wrapped
Anger toward you, trapped!

"Man, do not mourn the web of spiders!
Love transcends the dark broom riders!
World-Tree spreads to reach all corners
Its fruit and flowers lift gloom from mourners!

"Two faces have I, malevolent…benevolent
World-spider and web, World-tree and love's bent
So smile at the moon, play broom and cat's tune
Sing in the dark, love fierce, know the Ark!"

Mold of Metal
Ark of Gretel
Gold of Goddess
Ink of Blackness
Crown of Creature
Hecate Nature

Times of tears
Rhymes for fears
Aims for effect
Gaimes of direct
Instance of pain
Constance for gain

DOG

Friend of man, his fame
Civilized, loyal, tame
Fenced-in, "heel," must not tarry!
Guard-gate, child-play, fetch and carry

Yes, dog…
But, dog…

Cerberus hound, baying of hell
Boatman's sound, barking death's knell
Hands fingers in maw, feeling tooth's claw
Dark bite like a saw, scream catching in craw

Light dog…
Dark dog…
Yet…dog

Loving dog, fierce dog, true friend and true foe
His function with man: to be and to know
Together they face the way of the world
Together they brace the dark Underworld.

Dog…
D-O-G…
G-O-D…
God.

Is God not in dog?
Servant and Master, clear bright and blurred fog
Is dog not in God?
Instinct, Taskmaster, unite in the rod

Dog…
God…
Man.

Together: soul nature, spirit and flesh
Together: dog-man, two being enmesh
Hecate, Hades, Hell and gnome
Kronos, Rhea, Heaven and home

CAT

All know the feline form,
Independent
Green witch eyes staring
Hearth's cold ice baring

All know cat-o-nine-norm,
Condescendent
Mouse-kiss, tease-trick, cruel-reeking
Narciss', paw-lick, self-seeking
We know

But do all know the other side?
Introversion
That cats will come when one meditates?
That cats give love in man's darkened state?

But do all know the witch's ride?
Transformation
That night-roam and inner work are soul-food?
That fight-gloom and spinner-irk are toll-mood?

We know.

L'ENVOI

And what, at last do the Gods select?
And what, at last do centers effect?
Why Psyche, of course, in her butterfly state
Yes, Psyche, of course, love's soul and love's mate

It is Psyche and Eros who go through the changes
It is Psyche and Eros who flew through the ranges
Of center to center, straight up and straight down
Of center to center, each glows with a crown

The Lord speaks in Gods and in animals, too
The Lord, most of all, speaks in me and in you
For we are the vessel of God's transformation
Yes, we are the vessel, no group and no nation

The soul and the spirit unite in the flesh
The soul and the spirit delight and enmesh
In man and in woman, alone and together
In man and in woman, God's stone and God's feather

For God is both matter and spirit, at end
For God is both changing and permanent
In centers is He, for soul and for wife
In centers is She, behold Tree of Life

This is the end of the work, Him
This is the end of the work, Hymn
This is the end of the work, Her
This is the end of the work, Sir
This is the end of the work, It
This is the end of the work, Writ

Some Other Titles From New Falcon Publications

Aha! The Sevenfold Mystery of the Ineffable Love   **–Aleister Crowley**
Bio-Etheric Healing   **–Trudy Lanitis**
Undoing Yourself With Energized Meditation and Other Devices
Secrets of Western Tantra: The Sexuality of the Middle Path
Dogma Daze   **–Christopher S. Hyatt, Ph.D.**
Rebels & Devils; The Psychology of Liberation
   –Edited by Christopher S. Hyatt, Ph.D.
Aleister Crowley's Illustrated Goetia
Sex Magic, Tantra & Tarot: The Way of the Secret Lover
Taboo: Sex, Religion & Magick   **–C. Hyatt, Ph.D., and DuQuette**
Pacts With The Devil
Urban Voodoo: A Beginner's Guide to Afro-Caribbean Magic
   –Jason Black and Christopher S. Hyatt, Ph.D.
The Psychopath's Bible   **–Christopher S. Hyatt, Ph.D., and Jack Willis**
Ask Baba Lon   **–Lon Milo DuQuette**
Aleister Crowley and the Treasure House of Images
–J.F.C. Fuller, Aleister Crowley, Lon Milo DuQuette and Nancy Wasserman
Enochian Sex Magic and How To Workbook
   –Aleister Crowley, Lon Milo DuQuette and Christopher S. Hyatt, Ph.D.
Enochian World of Aleister Crowley   **–DuQuette and Aleister Crowley**
Info-Psychology
Neuropolitique
The Game of Life
What Does WoMan Want?   **–Timothy Leary, Ph.D.**
Rebellion, Revolution and Religiousness   **–Osho**
Reichian Therapy: A Practical Guide for Home Use   **–Dr. Jack Willis**
Woman's Orgasm: A Guide to Sexual Satisfaction
   –Benjamin Graber, M.D., and Georgia Kline-Graber, R.N.
Shaping Formless Fire
Seizing Power
Taking Power   **–Stephen Mace**
The Illuminati Conspiracy: The Sapiens System **–Donald Holmes, M.D.**
An Insider's Guide to Robert Anton Wilson   **–Eric Wagner**
The Secret Inner Order Rituals of the Golden Dawn   **–Pat Zalewski**
Hinduism and Jungian Psychology
Psycho-Mythology Series:
  The Tree, The Knight, and The Quest
The Wisdom of J. Marvin Spiegelman, Vol. 1- Selected Writings
The Wisdom of J. Marvin Spiegelman, Vol. II- Religion and Psychology
Sufism, Islam and Jungian Psychology   **–J. Marvin Spiegelman, Ph.D.**
Nonlocal Nature: The Eight Circuits of Consciousness
   –James A. Heffernan
on What is   **–Ja Wallin**

NEW FALCON PUBLICATIONS

**Publisher of Controversial Books and CDs
Invites you to visit our website
www.newfalcon.com**

- Browse the online catalog of all our great titles, including books by Israel Regardie, Christopher S. Hyatt, Robert Anton Wilson, Aleister Crowley, Timothy Leary, Osho, Lon Milo DuQuette and many more.
- Get special discounts
- Order our titles through our secure online server
- Find products not available anywhere else
    - One of a kind and limited availabiity products
    - Special packages
    - Special pricing
- And much, more more